Lorenzo!

The Restaurateur Who
Revolutionized an Industry

Lorenzo!

The Restaurateur Who Revolutionized an Industry

by Steve Reinertsen

solificatio

San Francisco, California

Lorenzo!
The Restaurateur Who Revolutionized an Industry

Copyright © 2025
by Larry Mindel and Steve Reinertsen
All rights reserved.

First Published by Solificatio
San Francisco, California
2025

ISBN: 979-8-9858781-8-9

Cover and interior book design by Solificatio
www.solificatio.com

Contents

1. Coffee Instants Incorporated 1
2. Caswell Coffee 11
3. Chianti 27
4. Early Spectrum 31
5. Full Spectrum 60
6. Open to It 70
7. Spectrum Takeout 90
8. Saga Sale 94
9. Early Il Fornaio 104
10. Branching Out 123
11. Il Fornaio Forges Forward 135
12. The Mille 138
13. Mixing Business with Pleasure 142
14. Moving On 146
15. Here Comes Hislop 149
16. Public and Private 159
17. Poggio 172
18. Copita 191
19. Convivo 197
20. Copita Willow Glen 204
21. Finito 208
22. Grazie 213

Coffee Instants Incorporated

Although many people think of Larry Mindel as a restaurateur, he got his start in the coffee business.

After graduating from The Ohio State University in the early 1930s, Larry's dad, Seymour, or Sy—known to many in the family as "Pa"—returned to Toledo and worked in his family's business. His father, Abraham, had established A. Mindel & Sons in 1913. The company bought and processed cattlehides that eventually became baseball covers or plush leather car seats.

In 1951, Sy's good friend Sidney Tuschman died suddenly, leaving behind his widow Helen and their fourteen-year-old twins, Joan and John. Sidney was a successful businessman and a prominent leader in the community. He and two partners had started an instant coffee processing plant in Long Island City, New York (Queens), utilizing new technology that had been developed in World War II. Helen did not know much about the business; New York was a long way from Toledo. After Sidney died, she asked Sy to go to New York, examine the business, and advise whether she should sell or hold her share.

When Sy returned from New York, he told Helen that the company, Coffee Instants Incorporated, was sound. She was pleased, but also wary about trying to help run a business she knew little about from six hundred miles away.

Sy offered to pay a fair price for Helen's share. She accepted.

Sy's life changed dramatically with that transaction; Larry's life changed as well. Until then, forty-year-old Sy had walked a predictable path, living where he grew up and working for the family company—an "awful" business according to Larry. He worked several summers in the tannery, where he endured the stench of curing hides firsthand.

Sy left A. Mindel & Sons—on good terms—and began a decades-long commute, flying from Toledo to New York on Monday mornings, returning home Friday afternoons. Larry was a freshman at Ottawa Hills High. He saw his father take a significant risk, hoping to make a better life for his family and for himself. Larry learned that everyone in the family had to sacrifice, to pay a price: he and his sister Carolyn missed their father when he was gone during the week; his mother, Ellie, missed her husband; and road warrior Sy missed the comforts of family and home.

Larry and father, Sy, annual summer fishing trip; Burleigh Falls, Canada

Those sacrifices, though painful at times, turned out to be worthwhile. Coffee Instants grew and prospered, and Sy eventually carved out a place for himself in the Big Apple. Perhaps the famous lyrics played prophetically in his head: "If I can make it there, I'll make it anywhere."

LAWRENCE BRISKER MINDEL
Class President 2,4; Class Vice-President 3; Boys' Chorus 2,3; Mixed Chorus 1,2,3; Hi-Y 2,3,4, Sergeant-at-Arms 4; Latin Club 1,2; Football 1,2,3,4; Basketball 1,2,3,4; Baseball 2,3,4; Golf 1; Intramurals 1,2,3; Council on World Affairs 4; Arrowhead 1,4; Mesasa Business Staff 4.

Ottawa Hills High School Class of 1955

Larry couldn't imagine a better place in the 1940s and '50s to grow up than Ottawa Hills, a small but lovely suburb of Toledo—despite experiencing overt antisemitism during his elementary school years: he was spit on while waiting for a Sunday School bus; some girls rebuffed his friendly advances; the (gentile) country club wanted Larry, who was a strong swimmer, to compete for their team but would not extend a junior membership. When Larry invited a school chum to play at his house, the boy declined, explaining, "I can't, you're Jewish." When an older and considerably taller and heavier soccer opponent called him a *kike*, Larry jumped on the ignorant behemoth's back and pounded his head, punch after punch. "No one ever called me that again," Larry later recalled.

The issue seemed to resolve itself by high school; perhaps the kids matured. Although perhaps slightly biased—after all, he did receive the school's Distinguished Alumnus Award in 2018, at which time he and his wife Debby established The Mindel Family Athletic Fund—Larry nevertheless deems Ottawa Hills High "the best public high school in Ohio, period."

Larry was a leader and an athlete during that wholesome, innocent time (for context, think the 1970s television series Happy Days). He was class president his freshman, sophomore, and senior years. By rule he could not serve as both junior class president and chair the prom; in a preview of things to come, he opted to host the party rather than participate in the student senate that year.

He was captain of the Green Arrow football and basketball teams. One Friday night, sporting the leather helmet—no face mask—that football players still wore then, Larry suffered a broken leg when recovering an onside kick. In spite of the injury, he played the entire third quarter. He didn't want his coach to think he was a "cake eater."

Larry, second from right, with school newspaper colleagues

When Larry and his pals weren't playing sports, they were over at Bob Snider's place working on their cars. Larry's first was his cousin

Tom Klein's 1941 coupe (dual mufflers, extremely loud exhaust cans). His "ultimate" was a 1938 Ford roadster with a full race Merc engine.

As he pulled up in front of school one morning, the roadster's engine caught fire. This ignominious entrance—a teacher ran out with a fire extinguisher to douse the blaze—did nothing to diminish Larry's high standing with the girls at school. He continued to enjoy preferred parking status at the local lovers' lane, where—given the far more innocent time and place—couples smooched for hours.

Larry and his buddies did not drink or smoke in high school, but they had plenty of high-spirited fun. Well before he was of driving age, Larry once "borrowed" his dad's car. When he returned home from that little joyride, Pete the Cop was waiting in the driveway.

When he realized Larry was out for an unsanctioned drive, his father called Pete. Pete knew everyone; everyone knew Pete. It was that kind of town. Sy felt that Pete could better deliver the necessary message. He was right.

"When I drove in and saw Pete standing there, arms folded tightly across his chest, he looked ten feet tall to me. I about crapped my pants," Larry recalled.

Pete's stern talking-to—no ticket—was nothing compared to Sy's silent treatment. After a few hours Larry cried out, "Please, Dad, anything but this!"

On another occasion, there were no significant repercussions when Larry and some pals hopped a freight train and rode it all the way to Chicago, 250 miles west. Good, clean fun.

Larry graduated from Ottawa Hills High in 1955 and enrolled at Washington and Lee University in Lexington, Virginia. The basketball coach had recruited him to play for the team. Larry very soon yearned for home; the "COLORED" water fountain in front of Lexington's Robert E. Lee Hotel bothered him greatly and strengthened this desire to return home.

His grades at W&L were uncharacteristically weak, which made transferring to his dream school, the University of Michigan, a challenge. As soon as Larry returned to Toledo for the summer, he drove the fifty miles north to Ann Arbor and sat down with the dean of admissions to discuss his situation. This was the first of what would turn out to be a lifetime of successful face-to-face conversations for Larry.

His willingness to admit that he had not given Washington and Lee his all and his determination to do whatever it took to be admitted to U of M impressed the dean, who exercised his administrative prerogative. If Larry went to summer school and earned at least a 3.75 grade point average he would be admitted to U of M, even though his Washington and Lee transcript did not meet traditional admission standards.

Larry went to summer school at the University of Toledo and hit the books hard. His GPA at the end of the term was 3.5; a substantial improvement, but still shy of the agreed-upon 3.75. Larry went back to the dean, presented his progress, and told him once again just how passionately he wanted to be a Wolverine. The dean saw something special in this technically unqualified young man and decided to bet on Larry.

Admitting him to the university was a gamble neither the administrator nor his colleagues or successors would regret. To the contrary, Michigan would eventually hold this accomplished and devoted alumnus in such high esteem that he'd be invited to speak on entrepreneurship at the business school.

First though, Larry had to get admitted.

He didn't assume he could coast through summer school then cruise on into Michigan. When, despite working extremely hard, he nonetheless came up a little short of the required mark, he didn't slink away with his tail between his legs. Larry's confidence made it natural for him to make a case for himself. He knew he was the cherished son of a successful businessman. He knew he was an accomplished athlete and a charismatic leader. He didn't expect special treatment, but he knew, even at that young age, the power of self-belief and how that confidence played in a personal meeting.

Larry enjoyed a productive and fulfilling three years at Michigan where he majored in English literature and minored in business. Reading F. Scott Fitzgerald "changed my life," he recalled. "That book taught me how to *dream*."

He had a good time with his ZBT fraternity brothers, including Charlie Helzberg, whose family owned Helzberg Diamonds, a jewelry retailer now boasting over 200 stores in thirty-six states. Another brother, Ira Harris, became a very successful investment banker. A devoted U of M football benefactor, he endowed the head coaching position and was Jim Harbaugh's agent.

Larry remembers one collegiate coming-of-age setback, when a young woman broke his heart by running off to Chicago with a law student. With nothing to go on other than a rough sense of where they lived, Larry made his way to Chicago. Amazingly, as he wandered their neighborhood, he came across his girlfriend and her new beau in a car. When she recognized him on the sidewalk, her face was overcome with shock. Lesson learned, Larry returned to Ann Arbor and was soon back in the game.

In the summer of 1959, following graduation from Michigan, Larry toured Europe with friends. He returned and moved to New York, where he began to work under his father and his father's two partners at Coffee Instants Incorporated.

Instant coffee was still quite new. Coffee Instants took raw green South or Central American coffee beans and cleaned, roasted, and ground them. They then mixed the ground product with hot water to brew an instant coffee precursor that was piped to a pulse combustion spray dryer. The dryer released liquid that was blown up and around towers at about 400 mph by air heated to 1000 degrees Fahrenheit. The water instantly evaporated, forming a powder—instant coffee—that collected at the bottom of the dryer.

Instant coffee made life simpler for the consumer. Merely by adding hot water and stirring, coffee was ready "instantly." Every bit of powder was absorbed—there were no leftover grounds. Americans were infatuated with convenience and labor-saving devices and products at that time, and instant coffee took off.

Coffee Instants manufactured their product in New York and shipped it via train to California, where they had a packaging plant in Burlingame, just south of the San Francisco airport. The West Coast supermarket chain Safeway was their biggest customer. In Burlingame, the subsidiary Western Coffee Instants (WCI) packaged the bulk coffee into jars or tins, affixed Safeway labels, and shipped cases to their stores all over the West.

One evening in New York, after the end of the workday, Larry's father and his partners were discussing possible troubles at the California packaging plant. No one knew for sure, but all three men sensed that something was off. The man they had running the operation might even be skimming money.

Larry, the young management trainee, sat quietly in a corner of the room, listening carefully. That was a big part of his job then, simply to listen and absorb as the older, more experienced businessmen met each day's challenges. This night was different.

"Let me go out there!" he impulsively told the men, breaking his usual silence. "I'll take a look and give you a full report."

Although he relished the opportunity to tackle the professional challenge the trip presented, he also really wanted to go to California. He had never been and "everyone" in the Midwest or East was excited about it.

"It was the place to be, the promised land. We listened to (pioneering surf sounders) Jan and Dean on the radio all the time," Larry later reminisced. Sy and his partners felt similarly. "It was my dad's proudest business moment, to have a plant in California."

Larry got his wish. The partners authorized him to fly to San Francisco to inspect the packaging plant.

He fell in love with California as soon as he stepped off the plane.

When Larry showed up at the plant, he introduced himself to John Alden, the man in charge, saying, "I'm here to help." Alden told him that he needed no help and slammed the door in Larry's face—not the most auspicious start.

Larry called his dad, and Sy and his two partners flew west. They fired Alden and discussed what to do next. Although selling WCI would break Sy's heart, given his love for California, from a business perspective it made sense.

Seeing an opportunity, Larry pleaded with the men to give him a shot at running Western Coffee Instants. The partners agreed. If, with just twelve thousand dollars operating capital, he could get the company running profitably within three months, he could stay; if he exceeded either of those limits, the experiment was over, and Larry would return to Queens. The partners already had a potential buyer lined up in Los Angeles.

Larry got to work immediately, calling on grocery chains throughout the West, establishing relationships with their buyers—primarily older men—and convincing them that Western Coffee Instants should be their supplier of choice.

To his surprise, Larry loved selling coffee. He enjoyed meeting buyers, and since he believed in his product, he truly felt he could help them prosper. Still the fierce standout athlete at heart, Larry loved the rush of high-stakes competition: if he didn't "win" enough sales calls in a very short period of time, Sy and his partners would sell Western Coffee Instants. Larry had fallen hard for California—San Francisco in particular—and had no desire to return to Coffee Instant's headquarters in Queens, his fate should he "lose" the WCI game.

With the help of two holdovers, a kind and competent secretary and a quiet but knowledgeable foreman, Larry met the partners' terms. He had WCI profitable within that crazy ninety-day timeframe, and he could stay in his now-beloved California. It was telling that the secretary and the foreman helped Larry, rather than undermining his efforts. A twenty-two-year-old owner's son in from elsewhere would be very easy to resent, if not even derail. But Larry had a way about him that drew people in.

Larry first rented a room at Baker's Acres, a thirteen-unit boardinghouse at the corner of Baker and Jackson Streets in Pacific Heights, one of San Francisco's tonier neighborhoods. "Baker's Acres" was emblazoned in script on the building's front awning. Many of the boardinghouse's residents were other young people just getting their start in the city. They hailed from all over the United States. Handsome and gregarious Larry made friends quickly. The residents all ate breakfast and dinner at a communal table and were always welcome at the legendary Friday night cocktail parties at the Pink Palace nearby on Scott Street.

Once Larry knew that he had WCI running smoothly enough to support more permanent housing, he "graduated" from Baker's Acres to an apartment at Green and Webster Streets, moving in with fellow Ohioans Jay Bass and Steve Gordon, as well as San Francisco bornand-bred Gary Goddard and Paul Diller.

Larry worked hard because he wanted to stay in California, and because he liked the challenge. He also enjoyed making money. More significantly, Larry wanted to justify his father's faith in him. Larry knew that Sy had taken a big chance when he gave a young man such a remarkable opportunity, and he wanted more than anything to repay his dad by succeeding.

One night after work at his apartment, Larry cracked open a beer and told Gary, "I called on George Caswell Coffee Company today. It's so old the accountants wear those green visor eyeshades, like in a movie! They turned me down. They don't want to carry our instant coffee, but I had the strangest feeling when I was there: I want to buy that company."

Caswell was not one of the Big Three roasters—Hills Bros., Folgers, or MJB—but it was no mom-and-pop either. It had been around forever.

Larry was twenty-four, and, although WCI was going and growing, his personal checking account showed a balance of thirty-six dollars that evening.

Gary said, "I know Caswell. My uncle's firm has handled their insurance for years. I can ask."

Three days later, Gary reported back that the company was not for sale. Larry shrugged. He was busy enough at WCI, and his wish to buy the roasting company soon faded. He could not afford it, so the refusal was no big deal.

Although he worked hard, Larry was also beginning to find time to socialize, so he had more on his mind than just instant coffee. Soon he was dating Mimi Marx, a cute little Cal coed three years his junior. Gary's girlfriend Yvonne Anixter was one of Mimi's Berkeley roommates. Everyone knew everyone back then, or so it felt.

Mimi graduated from Cal in May of 1962. She and Larry were married in Toledo on November 19 of that same year. He was twenty-five, she was twenty-two. They had a small family wedding. Mimi's dad, Sonny, and her sister-in-law, Gayle, flew back to Toledo with Larry and Mimi and were in attendance along with Larry's parents when the young sweethearts made it official.

After they returned from Toledo, Larry and Mimi lived briefly in a Laurel Heights apartment on Anza Street, before moving into the house that Mimi would occupy for over fifty years at 465 Avila in the Marina.

Caswell Coffee

One Friday Larry got a call at work. A deep voice asked, "Mr. Mindel?" No one had ever called Larry that before in his life. After looking around for his father, Larry replied, "Yes, this is he."

"I understand you want to buy my company. The board has agreed to sell. The price is one million dollars. If you are interested, be in my office at eight o'clock on Monday morning," growled Caswell's chief executive officer, George Malmgren.

A stunned Larry—he had dropped his Caswell dream once Gary Goddard relayed word that the company was not for sale—met Malmgren at Caswell that Monday. They didn't get very far, but as Larry was leaving Malmgren did say, "We'll meet again."

Larry could not believe that this wish he had shared in passing with his roommate, almost as a joke, might now come true. Once he realized that he actually might be able to buy the company, he did not hesitate. He wanted it badly. He asked himself, "Where will I get a million bucks?" *The bank*, he thought, answering his own question. *You get the money from a bank. That's what banks are for. They have money.*

Larry's father, whom he loved and respected, was an experienced businessman and still technically his boss. Although Larry ran Western Coffee Instants on a day-to-day basis, his father and his New York partners owned the company; Sy was president of WCI, Larry vice president. Some might have expected Larry to call his dad before doing anything else, but his first move was to try to make it on his own. He loved and idolized his father, but in a spirit of self-belief, self-respect, and adventure, he decided to try to raise the money himself.

Off to the banks he went. He started at what was then Bank of America's main branch on Montgomery Street. He did not get to speak to anyone of significance there; a careful junior associate gave him a bland corporate brushoff. The same thing happened at Wells Fargo,

Union Bank, and the Bank of California. But Larry persisted. Finally, at Pacific National Bank, which later became Security Pacific Bank before ultimately being swallowed up by Bank of America in 1992, a man named Al Cinelli invited Larry to give his pitch.

Al was a classic San Franciscan, the son of Italian immigrants Giuseppe and Elvira Cinelli. According to his *San Francisco Chronicle* obituary, "a prolific banker and sports fan within the City, (Al) was proud to have banked the early years of the San Francisco Forty Niners, San Francisco Giants, and the San Francisco Warriors."

Larry explained that through his work with Western Coffee Instants he had built a good reputation with the region's largest supermarket-chain buyers and was confident that he could convince them to add Caswell's roasted coffee to their orders. And, if he were able to buy Caswell, he could move WCI's operations from the leased Burlingame location into Caswell's bigger building. While this wouldn't guarantee a certain profit, it would at least insure against a disastrous loss.

Al was intrigued by this idea, but more importantly, similar to the University of Michigan admissions officer, he *liked* Larry immediately and apparently saw something special in the ambitious young executive. He asked Larry if a bank were to lend him the money, how he would pay it back.

Larry thought for a moment and admitted that he hadn't gotten quite that far yet. Cinelli chuckled and said that if Larry ever hoped to secure a loan, he would need to be able to convince the bank that he had a viable repayment plan. Larry needed a business plan, and Cinelli coached him on what that entailed. He offered to review whatever Larry produced.

Selling instant coffee by day, at night Larry sat at his dining room table writing a business plan. He returned to Pacific National several times, and each time Cinelli reviewed Larry's progress and suggested logical next steps.

After a half dozen of these tutorials, Cinelli announced, "Here's what I'm going to do. I will lend you $350,000 as a first mortgage against the Caswell building, which the company owns outright. I will offer you an additional $350,000 unsecured loan, because I like you and I believe in you. Plus, if you clear out the third floor and move Western Coffee Instants in there and charge them rent, that represents some solidity. The final $300,000 will be up to you. You will need to raise that yourself."

Thrilled to get the bulk of the loan, but having never solicited any private capital in his life, Larry nonetheless set about trying to raise the remaining $300,000 (almost $3,000,000 in 2025 dollars).

Proud of his solo efforts to date, Larry now felt comfortable telling his father and father-in-law about his Caswell dream. Both men were impressed with Larry's moxie and offered to help. San Francisco native Sonny knew many accomplished businessmen in town. He made introductions and Larry took it from there. His WCI experience and success, the sound plan Cinelli had helped him formulate, and the $700,000 Pacific National had already committed impressed several of these men enough not only to invest, but also to accept Larry's request to serve on his nascent but stacked board of directors.

On August 16, 1965, the *San Francisco Chronicle* reported the following:

> One of San Francisco's oldest family-owned companies has changed hands and changed names, it was announced today.
>
> Purchased by a group of investors headed by Laurence B. Mindel, vice president of Western Coffee Instants, and including some of California's best-known businessmen, the George W. Caswell Company, processors of institutional and consumer coffee since 1884, is now the Caswell Coffee Company. Purchase price was not revealed but was 'within the seven numbers figure,' according to a spokesman.
>
> Laurence B. Mindel assumes presidency of the new firm. Among the purchasers and serving with Mindel on the new Board of Directors are:
>
> Louis Petri, president, United Vintners; Stanton Sobel, president, House of Sobel; Ben Brite, president, Western States Insurance Brokers; Melville [Sonny] Marx, partner, J. Barth & Co.; Donald Pritzker, president, Hyatt House Hotels; Seymour [Sy] Mindel, president, Western Coffee Instants; and Frederick Weisman, former president of Hunt Foods.
>
> Plant and offices will remain at 642 Harrison St., San Francisco.

Some context and background on the board members: Petri's United Vintners joined Heublein in 1968; a $33 million merger (roughly $280 million today). Some Pritzkers live in Marin, others in Chicago (JB Pritzker is currently governor of Illinois). Hunt Foods was a large nationwide brand focused mostly on ketchup. Weisman was a noted art collector who also made headlines when he clashed with Frank Sinatra one night at the Beverly Hills Hotel Polo Lounge. Sinatra, who was helping Dean Martin celebrate his forty-ninth birthday, reportedly threw a telephone at Weisman, fracturing his skull.

Larry would later laugh recalling the mortgage piece of the loan, because the building's collateral value hadn't entered his mind until Cinelli mentioned it; he was that green. Today it would be one of the first things he would see if he were considering an acquisition.

The Pacific National loan would not have happened had Larry not walked into the bank. Cinelli had to be able to get a feel for Larry, and that best happens—maybe *only* happens—live, in person.

Larry picked up a cashier's check for one million dollars at Pacific National and took it to Caswell to complete the sale.

"I felt dizzy," he said. "My thought after I walked in the Caswell door—Caswell, which was now *my* company—and saw the green-visored accountants with their adding machines and ledger books, and the rough-looking truck drivers and men who ran the roasters and grinders and vacuum packing machines was, *How will I, at twenty-seven, get all these people to follow me?*"

He wasn't the complete rookie he had been at Western Coffee Instants. He delegated and managed, but he also still called on customers and potential customers and sold. He convinced some existing WCI accounts to continue to buy their instant product, but also to add Caswell roasted coffee to their orders.

Many notable San Francisco restaurants, like Ernie's and Enrico's, served Caswell coffee. Larry especially enjoyed servicing those accounts. He met owners and managers, including Victor and Roland Gotti and Enrico Banducci, and began to feel at home in their establishments. These were new work environments for Larry: WCI sold primarily to grocery stores. Restaurants did not typically serve instant coffee, offering diners roasted coffee instead. As proud as Larry was of Coffee Instants, when he bought Caswell he was moving up the prestige ladder; roasted coffee was generally held in higher esteem than instant.

Larry took pride in Caswell's quality—quality that the firm assured through daily tastings. Many mornings Larry would join Caswell's coffee buyer and three or four other key operations men in the cupping room. They would batch roast and grind a small sample of that day's beans, then pour hot water over the grounds into small cups. After letting the coffee cool for a few minutes, the men would taste the brew, letting it linger on their tongues as they evaluated aroma, acidity, sweetness, mouthfeel, aftertaste, and balance, before depositing that taste into an old-fashioned brass spittoon.

Caswell bought green beans from the three or four major San Francisco coffee importers, receiving fresh shipments several days a week. Each coffee harvest is different, even if beans are sourced from the same Central American farm. Weather, altitude, soil—all impact the taste of a particular batch. Since Caswell sought to deliver the same consistent, distinctive quality taste to their customers, shipment after shipment, they tasted daily and blending accordingly.

In 1925 Caswell built a three-story reinforced concrete building—a combined plant, warehouse, and office—at 642 Harrison Street, at Hawthorne. It was an industrial building, in an industrial part of town. Larry's grandchildren have since driven past it hundreds of times on the way to Giants games.

Caswell sponsored basketball and bowling teams. A November 1, 1967, *San Francisco Chronicle* sports page brief reported that the previous evening Liberty Radiator beat "hapless" Caswell Coffee three games to none at L&L Castle Lanes.

Today 642 Harrison is home to a tech company, Highline Platforms. People there were extremely warm and gracious when Larry visited unexpectedly in spring of 2022. He went with a friend to see whether the big brass doors he remembered remained today. Ever the aesthete, he believed they were simply a nice architectural flourish; someone who sees the world through slightly darker lenses might suspect that Caswell, like Hills Brothers, installed brass doors as a security measure ahead of the 1934 waterfront strike.

Larry didn't see the brass doors, but as he peered through the frosted front glass a very nice woman appeared and asked if she could help. Larry proudly announced that he used to own the building.

She smiled and said, "Oh, really? When was that?"

"Sixty years ago!" he crowed.

The woman invited him in and gave him a tour.

Caswell Coffee and Highline Platforms could not have been more different. When Larry owned the company, longshoremen unloaded the heavy burlap bags of Central or South American beans from the holds of ships docked at the nearby piers. The bags were then trucked to adjacent coffee importers' warehouses. Caswell, like Hills Brothers down the street at 2 Harrison, MJB at Third and Townsend, and Folger's at 101 Howard, bought truckloads of green coffee beans from the importers. Caswell would then roast, grind, blend, package, and distribute their premium product. It was loud, messy—if aromatic—blue-collar work.

In contrast, Highline was clean and quiet, with all the modern tech-company amenities: neon signs on the walls proclaiming values like "customer obsessed"; an open floor plan ringed by meeting rooms named after recording studios like Abbey Road and The Record Plant, even though Highline's business had nothing to do with music; and an in-house café, heavy on plant-based offerings.

The tour highlight for Larry was seeing the room that had once been his office.

"My desk was here," he said enthusiastically, "and over there was the bar!"

He went on to recall the camaraderie that grew not only out of working hard toward a shared goal but also from end-of-workday martinis, nice follow-ups to the ones he and his team enjoyed at lunch at the venerable House of Shields, a block and half away on New Montgomery. Established in 1908, it had no clocks or TVs.

As Larry said goodbye to the woman, he requested her business card. He wanted to drop her boss a note telling him just how welcoming and helpful she had been, what a fine ambassador she was for Highline. She giggled, shook her head apologetically, and, putting a finger to her lips as a hush, said, "We don't have those anymore." The implication was clear: *No one gives out cards today, honored elder, everything's digital!* Larry could only laugh as he shuffled back outside, where many of the passing cars were a self-driving vehicle.

The Caswell years were a busy, anxious time for Larry, during which he worked extremely hard. "Uneasy lies the head that wears a crown," Shakespeare wrote. Employees, investors, and his young, growing family—his son Michael was fifteen months when Larry bought the company, and his daughter Laura was born just seven months later—all counted on him to succeed.

Larry convinced Sol Price of FedMart to carry Caswell coffee. Price, considered a pioneer in the "warehouse store" retail model, later founded Price Club, which merged with Costco in 1993. Sam Walton wrote in his book *Made In America* that he "borrowed" as many ideas from Price as from anyone else, including Sol's suffix, resulting in the name Walmart.

Larry also persuaded another interesting southern California business, Helms Bakery, to sell Caswell coffee to their residential customers. Helms operated on a large scale, offering more than 150 items—loaves, rolls, doughnuts, cookies, and even milk and butter—but none were sold in stores. Helms's motto was "Daily at Your Door," and every weekday morning dozens of Helms delivery trucks—similar to those driven by the milkmen of Michael and Laura's youth—would leave the large industrial bakery for parts of Los Angeles. When the truck drivers pulled on a large handle, a distinctive whistle alerted customers to come out and buy still-warm baked goods. Larry thought Caswell would be an ideal complement. Helms agreed.

So eager was Larry to land this high-profile account that when he learned that owner Paul Helms wanted to sell his boat, Larry bought it. This was the birth of Larry the Yachtsman.

Prior to that, boat ownership was not high on Larry's list of priorities. Truth be told, it wasn't on his list at all—and he didn't have a wad of cash burning a hole in his pocket either. But when he heard Helms say he wanted to sell, the scrappy entrepreneur, wanting to ingratiate himself with a big would-be customer, responded like an impulsive, playful kid. Even before his wife knew, Larry owned a 32' wooden lapstrake hull boat, which he presciently renamed *Espresso*.

That spontaneous purchase, like so many of Larry's other seat-of-the-pants decisions, worked out beautifully. He owned a succession of boats for the next fifty years, and today counts every hour he spent aboard them among the best of his life.

Caswell already sold a small amount of premium Kona coffee. After he bought the company, Larry began attending the annual coffee roasters association convention at the Pebble Beach Hotel in Monterey. It was natural for him to socialize with men from the Kona Growers Association. In welcome contrast to older, stuffier San Francisco coffee titans like Peter Folger and Reuben Wilmarth Hills III, who simply would not speak to him, the Kona men lived *aloha*, bringing with them that beautiful Big Island warmth.

One year at the convention, the Kona growers told Larry they were in trouble. Their labor force was shrinking at an alarming rate, as workers left demanding field jobs for easier gigs in the new hotels opening throughout the islands. One example was the Mauna Kea Beach Hotel, which opened in July of 1965, just a month before Larry bought Caswell.

On top of that, the Big Three in San Francisco—Hills Bros., Folger's, and MJB—had all the leverage over the growers. The companies used relatively small amounts of the premium Kona beans to enrich their overall blends, but they were still the growers' biggest customers. They could basically name their price. The growers feared that a dwindling labor supply and ever-thinner profit margins might drive them under, even forcing the Kona coffee industry to disappear altogether.

Larry listened to his friends' woes and offered a suggestion. He knew that the Big Three used premium Colombian coffee in the same way they used Kona, an expensive, sparingly added seasoning. To Larry's mind, Kona coffee was just as good as Colombian coffee, but Hills, Folger's, and MJB were paying a lot more for the latter than for the former, due in part perhaps to superior Colombian marketing. The Doyle Dane Bernbach advertising agency, working for the National Federation of Coffee Growers of Colombia, had created Juan Valdez, a fictional character, who, along with his donkey Conchita, helped give the impression that Colombian coffee was superior.

Larry advised the Kona growers to raise their price to ten percent less than their Colombian competitors, as listed each day in the *Journal of Commerce*. Kona would still be cheaper than Colombian, but the growers could make more money, hopefully enticing more Big Island farmers to stay in or even enter the coffee business.

The growers were afraid the ruthless Big Three would stop buying if they raised the price. Larry assured them that wouldn't happen.

"Kona is a great product, with a great name," he insisted. "It's got sex appeal!"

The growers invited him to Hawaii. They wanted their fellow farmers to meet this intriguing and enterprising young *haole* from San Francisco and consider his proposal. Larry flew to Kona—the airport was basically just a shack back then—and took questions from the Kona Growers Association. Repeating the price-structure recommendation he had made at Pebble Beach, he boldly added, "And I will buy whatever you don't sell at your new price, whatever's left over." The growers went quiet and looked at each other.

"Really?" one asked.

"Really," said Larry.

They made a deal right then and there, on the spot, with a handshake—not a single written word. Those were the days.

Flying home to San Francisco, Larry felt like throwing up.

What the hell did I just do? he asked himself. He was on the hook for whatever the Kona Growers Association didn't sell. *What am I going to do now?*

As always, the answer was to get out there and sell.

He started with airport gift shops, convincing several to carry Caswell Kona Coffee in attractively designed tins. That wasn't the volume Larry needed to move, but apparently the menehune-like coffee gods saw him hustling as only a young, "scared shitless" (Larry's words) family man could. After months of uncertainty and effort, the gods provided Larry a possible path forward.

Someone—likely a fellow Young Presidents Organization (YPO) member—put him in touch with Harold Butler, the founder and CEO of Denny's Restaurants. In that pre-Starbucks era, Denny's was the largest coffee shop chain in America. As they talked, Larry realized Butler wanted to upgrade the "quality image" of Denny's. Larry pounced.

"I can upgrade your image through coffee. I think you'll agree, right now your house coffee is less than mediocre. If you replace it with Caswell Kona, people will say it's the best cup of coffee they have ever had."

Butler, like so many of the men with whom Larry did business at the time, was at least fifteen years older. More often than not, twenty-eight-year-old Larry was dealing with men in their mid-forties. This required incredible confidence. But Butler and Larry came to like, trust, and respect each other. Soon after Butler sampled Caswell Kona the two men made a deal, one that Larry bluntly explained, "saved my ass."

Although unclear on the exact amount, Larry recalled Denny's buying more than 100,000 pounds of Caswell Kona that year. Whatever the amount, they bought out the entire supply.

"Everybody won," Larry explained. "Denny's won, the Kona growers won, and Caswell won, too."

Larry's Caswell purchase had qualified him for membership in the Young Presidents Organization. At that time a prospective member needed to be under forty years of age and to head a company with at least fifty employees and more than one million dollars in annual sales. Caswell employed sixty people, with distribution centers in Los Angeles, Sacramento, San Jose, Watsonville, Honolulu, and San Diego.

LAURENCE B. MINDEL is President and Chief Executive Officer of Caswell Foods, Inc., with a thorough business background that belies his youthful years and qualifies him as an outstanding member of the Young President's Organization of Northern California, International.

YPO: The First Fifty Years (2000) describes the organization as "a forum of highly motivated peers, driven, eager to learn, and willing to share experiences openly, in camaraderie, trust and respect." It describes members as "people with gifts of creativity, intelligence, inexhaustible energy and stubborn individualism, who believe that business in the 'incentive state' as opposed to the 'hand-out' state is the best business for everyone."

Larry attended annual YPO meetings across the country and later throughout the world, including Egypt, Cuba, and Turkey. He also met monthly with his home chapter, which included sages like Gary Rodgers (Dryers Ice Cream), Art Ciocca (The Wine Group), and Dino Cortopassi (Stanislaus Food Products, Muir Glen Organic Tomatoes). YPO was a place where young business leaders could share honestly their special challenges. Other members understood as only those on a similar path could. They knew what it was like to be young and sometimes doubted, resented, or not taken seriously. Members could offer each other possible solutions to problems, based on their own similar experiences.

As one member commented, "It was exhilarating and uplifting, in the sense of what you were learning, the ideas you were exchanging, and feeling comfortable with these (high-powered) people."

YPO: The First Fifty Years includes a similar observation: "Many members shared an emotional attachment to YPO because it offered them a network to offset the feelings of personal isolation many of them experienced as the head of their firm…At YPO you are talking to people with the same worries and you can let your hair down. Somehow, YPO allowed them to think that reaching out for help from each other was not a sign of weakness but of strength."

That final sentence bears repeating, especially for younger readers, applying as it does across the board, in any situation, occupational or personal.

In the late 1960s, Larry and his father found themselves in an interesting situation. Sy's New York company, Coffee Instants Incorporated, was struggling.

Sy was Larry's idol. Watching his father take risks and succeed had made it natural for Larry to attempt things that others would not. He believed in Sy's ability to right the Coffee Instants ship, given a bit more time and operating capital. To provide his father both, he told the Caswell board he wanted to buy the company. They approved the acquisition.

Some very experienced and savvy businessmen sat on Caswell's board. They would not have approved the Coffee Instants acquisition if it were a reckless move. All the same, it did make for some uncomfortable moments.

One morning Larry lost patience with his dad. Larry needed to bring Coffee Instants's numbers to that afternoon's Caswell board meeting. He had asked Sy for the figures several times, but Sy had put him off. Larry felt under the gun: the Caswell board members were gentlemen, but they were also businessmen. At a certain point they were going to demand the information, data that Larry—who ultimately served at their pleasure—had yet to obtain. Larry got his dad on the line and barked, "Come on, Dad, I need the effing numbers!"

Sy paused before replying, "Don't you ever speak to me that way. You may temporarily outrank me in this unique situation, but I am still your father. You will never speak to me that way again."

Larry knew Sy was right. Chagrined, he apologized to his father.

The story had the happiest of endings a few months later when Chock full o'Nuts, a large New York coffee company, bought Coffee Instants from Caswell. Sy became president of Chock as part of the deal. He thrived in that high-profile role, still commuting weekly from Toledo to New York. (Legend has it the flight attendants liked him so much and knew his schedule so well that they would hold the plane for him.)

Sometime in 1969 or 1970, at the same Pebble Beach coffee convention where the Kona deal had come together, Chicago-based Superior Coffee and Tea's president surprised Larry, asking if he would consider selling Caswell. Superior was creating a gourmet division and coveted Caswell's Kona connection. Although Larry had not bought Caswell with the idea of selling it after just four or five years, as president he had a responsibility to his investors to listen when the suitor approached.

The deal came together quickly. Investors were delighted, and Larry himself was pleased—if a little stunned—too. By the ripe old age of thirty-three he had bought, grown, and now sold a bona fide company.

The terms of the sale stipulated that Larry continue to run Caswell for two more years; common practice then and now. Larry started out doing just that. However, not long into the new setup, he flew to Chicago and told Mr. Cohn, Superior's president, he could not continue.

Larry's father and Chock full o'Nuts president, Sy Mindel, center, with actors Alan Arkin and Peter Falk, filming *The In-Laws* at a Chock shop in New York City, 1978.

Larry's heretofore quite traditional wife, Mimi, got caught up in San Francisco's post-Summer of Love find-yourself scene. Without warning, she decided she wanted a freer life. She began spending less time at home in the Marina and more time at Stinson Beach, where she devoted herself to an exploration of the alternative lifestyle in vogue at the time.

For the next few years, Larry often had to play a role he had never imagined: single father to three young children. It quickly became too much. The constant pit in his stomach told him he was failing both his children and his employer, unable to uphold the very high standards he had for himself. A man before his time, he boldly put family first and reluctantly gave Superior seventy-two-hour notice, forfeiting what remained of the thirty-six thousand dollar salary he had so proudly negotiated for himself.

"I was a wreck," he later recollected. "It did not end well for me, nor did it end well for Superior. There was no one to run the company."

Larry worked hard to stabilize his chaotic family situation. He would later look back on the first three years of his and Mimi's split as the most significant of his life.

"It was such an important time. We were all together, just the three kids and me, hiking, backpacking, fishing. It's all I knew how to do besides take them to school. They provided so much emotional enrichment—I needed them more than they needed me. Losing and feeling rejected by someone were new experiences for me. And I wasn't used to the responsibility of taking care of kids. But the four of us had this connection. I knew we were a team, a family."

Larry eventually came to terms with Mimi's quest for freedom and adventure—a decision for which she later expressed some remorse—deeming it understandable given the time and place.

Chianti

Once Larry's turbulent family situation stabilized, he began to think about what to do next.

Although he had made a nice profit on the Caswell sale—in the area of $100,000, or about $780,000 in 2025 dollars—it wasn't enough for a young and energetic father of three youngsters to retire (particularly for a man who, despite being financially secure, would continue heading into the office most days into his late eighties).

As he evaluated his years at Caswell, he realized that though the positives far outweighed the negatives, he had felt somewhat isolated running the company—it had been "lonely at the top." He had interacted regularly with employees and customers, but moving ahead he hoped to experience more connection and collaboration and less isolation.

Personable and outgoing, Larry had made many friends during his first ten years in San Francisco. When one friend, Jerry Magnin, a San Franciscan who had moved to Los Angeles, mentioned to another friend, Steve Goddard, that he was thinking about buying a restaurant, Steve—who worked in finance—replied that restaurants were notoriously terrible investments. He suggested that Jerry instead talk to Larry, who was looking for his next challenge. Maybe a restaurant would be the right fit.

Jerry worked for his family's business. In 1919 his grandfather, Joseph, had left his father Isaac's thriving San Francisco-based I. Magnin Company to found The Joseph Magnin Company, an upscale clothier. (Coincidentally, Mimi's mother, Louise, had once been an I. Magnin fashion model, considered by many at the time to be among the most beautiful women in San Francisco.)

Initially, Joseph Magnin existed in the shadow of the better-established and more exclusive I. Magnin. That changed after World War

II, when Jerry's dad, Cyril, "elevated the brand," perhaps best illustrated by Marilyn Monroe's choice of a Joseph Magnin suit for her 1954 marriage to Joe DiMaggio.

Jerry worked for Joseph Magnin throughout the 1960s, in both San Francisco and Los Angeles. In 1969 Cyril sold the company to Hawaii-based Amfac, which owned Liberty House department stores.

One day in 1970, Jerry called Larry, telling him to fly down to Los Angeles as soon as possible. One of Jerry's favorite restaurants, Chianti, would soon be sold in an estate sale. Dubious but intrigued, not long after Larry found himself dining with Jerry at Chianti.

Chianti opened on Melrose Avenue in the late 1930s. Hollywood stars like Cary Grant, Spencer Tracy, and Humphrey Bogart appreciated what one writer called "its reserved, romantic old-world atmosphere…discreet high-backed booths, low light level, attentive waiters…" The *Gone with the Wind* cast party was rumored to have been held at Chianti in 1938.

By 1970 the restaurant had seen better days. There were only six other diners the night Larry and Jerry had their fateful dinner. Nevertheless, by their second—or perhaps third—bottle of wine, the pair—with zero restaurant industry experience between them—had fallen in love with Chianti. They wanted to buy the venerable, if fading, *ristorante*.

Larry ran the idea past his father. Sy advised against it, telling Larry what the younger man already knew: an overwhelming majority of new restaurants fail within the first year. As a New Yorker, Sy also couldn't help but connect Italian restaurants with the Mafia. He lovingly expressed paternal concern for Larry's reputation and, even, safety.

This was difficult for Larry to hear. He idolized his father, both as a man and as an accomplished executive. Despite his father's advice, however, his gut still told him to buy the restaurant. Sy understood and wished Larry well.

Jerry and Larry knew themselves well enough to send an attorney to negotiate the purchase. They wanted Chianti fiercely, but they didn't want to overpay.

They were beyond disappointed when the seller rebuffed their inquiry. The widow was selling the restaurant but planned to hold onto the building. Her insurance company was raising her rates based on the substantial square footage of the building's storefront windows. She hoped to lease the building to a drugstore, which could wall over most, if not all, of the windows, lowering her insurance bill.

A few days later, a woman called Jerry and asked if he was related to Isaac Magnin. Her question felt strange. He warily replied yes, Isaac was his grandfather. The woman went on to explain that her father had worked for him at I. Magnin and that Isaac was a "wonderful man." She was willing to sell the restaurant to "you boys," rather than holding out for the drugstore of her premium-lowering dreams. On such small connections and breaks do entire companies, careers, and lives sometimes hinge.

The attorney handled the details from there. Larry and Jerry bought the restaurant for $24,000 (about $190,000 in 2025). They closed it for a month and spent another $12,000 improving the interior, changing the menu, and hiring an Italian chef "right off the boat," vowing to make it the best Italian restaurant in California. They would serve *real* Italian food, rather than American-Italian spaghetti and meatballs.

Jerry traveled to Italy regularly, both growing up and in his work for Joseph Magnin; his early vision was invaluable in helping to chart the course. Larry caught up soon enough.

When Chianti opened for business, Larry and Jerry assumed it would be packed. Each had experienced success in his twenties. They both believed in not only each other, but also their concept and people.

The restaurant got off to a slow start. Larry couldn't sleep, fretting that the money he'd made from the Caswell sale would spiral down the drain. Initial press coverage skewed more salacious than savory: when Chianti's bookkeeper found out his wife was having an affair with the restaurant manager, he lured the manager outside and shot him to death.

Larry's family life wasn't much more relaxed. He lived and worked in Los Angeles during the week and flew to San Francisco to care for Michael, Laura, and Tony on the weekends. They were seven, five, and two. Mimi was still "finding herself," so Larry couldn't single-mindedly devote himself to work, secure in the knowledge that his children were in a stable situation. Often they were, sometimes they were not. Larry couldn't help but worry.

As the restaurant lost money, Larry began to question whether he should have listened to his father, who had advised against the venture. Maybe Larry and Jerry didn't have the Midas touch they thought they had. Regardless, Larry was in too deep to pull out now; all he and Chianti could do was keep going, day by day.

Just when failure appeared imminent, the phone began to ring. It didn't stop ringing for the next fifteen years. Unbeknownst to Larry, Lois Dwan, the influential *Los Angeles Times* food critic—as powerful as any in the United States outside of New York—had eaten incognito at Chianti earlier that week. Not only was it the best Italian restaurant in Los Angeles, she wrote, it might well be the best restaurant of *any kind* in the city.

Dwan's review saved Chianti. Celebrities soon "fought for tables," while other patrons sometimes had to plead for reservations. The restaurant began to thrive, and Larry and Jerry quickly regained their temporarily shaken confidence.

One day Jerry learned from his father, Cyril, that his friend and Democratic power broker, Walter Shorenstein, had teamed with New Jersey-based Mutual Benefit Life Insurance Company to develop a thirty-two-story office building at 5900 Wilshire Boulevard. Directly across from the Los Angeles County Museum of Art, it was also just two miles from Chianti.

There would be restaurant space in the building's plaza. Emboldened by Chianti's success and his father's suggestion, Jerry broached with Larry the possibility of a second restaurant—something completely different, not another Chianti—at 5900 Wilshire.

Jerry invited several Los Angeles investors to join their new venture, which they called the Spectrum Foods company.

Early Spectrum

There was never a grand plan to build a multi-restaurant company.

"We didn't even have a plan for Chianti, let alone anything beyond," Larry explained. "We were just winging it."

But opportunity appeared to be knocking. Jerry, in particular, wanted to capitalize.

The Green House restaurant, along with the Potting Shed annex, became Jerry's passion project, his hometown baby. Looking back, from Larry's perspective they might have placed too much emphasis on eclectic décor and not enough on food. "It just wasn't grounded enough," he later reflected, shaking his head and chuckling as he recalled the German chef—meat cleaver in hand—chasing a waiter around the fancy continental restaurant.

Whatever its faults, The Green House was the first of what would come to be sixteen post-Chianti Spectrum Foods restaurants. Without the opportunity to expand that Spectrum provided, Larry's story might have turned out quite differently.

Larry's heart—his family—was still in San Francisco. Naturally, he began to dream of a Spectrum restaurant in that very promising market, a place that would be "his," just as The Green House was Jerry's. The restaurant would require a fair amount of hands-on management, meaning that Larry would work in San Francisco as much as or even more than Los Angeles. As a dedicated father, he relished that prospect. *What would be best for Michael, Laura, and Tony?* ran constantly through his head. His immediate priority was his kids, since Mimi's new life no longer included him as her husband.

The divorce initiated another period of transition. It took time for Larry to accept and manage what he came to see as rejection. He had won consistently in life to this point, so he was ill-prepared for a loss of this magnitude. He had not wanted to break up the family, and he loved Mimi.

There was also the matter of pride. Intellectually, he knew that Mimi's choices were not necessarily a criticism of him. But his competitive gut wanted to show Mimi that he could be just as *meshuga*, i.e., crazy, out there, hip, as she. Part of him hoped to prove she was wrong to leave.

While that longing wasn't his only motivation, it strongly influenced Larry's vision for the San Francisco restaurant. He wanted to create a place that Mimi would like, a place that would open her eyes to just how hip one Laurence B. Mindel of Toledo, Ohio could be.

"MacArthur Park," a Grammy-winning song that peaked at number two on the *Billboard Hot 100* in 1968, just ahead of Simon & Garfunkel's "Mrs. Robinson," still got regular airplay in 1972. It pulled at Larry's heartstrings and became a touchstone as he brainstormed the San Francisco restaurant. Songwriter Jimmy Webb said that "The territory I tend to inhabit is that sort of 'crushed lonely hearts' thing."

> *MacArthur Park is melting in the dark*
> *All the sweet, green icing flowing down*
> *Someone left the cake out in the rain*
> *I don't think that I can take it*
> *'Cause it took so long to bake it*
> *And I'll never have that recipe again*
> *Oh, no*
>
> *I recall the yellow cotton dress*
> *Foaming like a wave*
> *On the ground beneath your knees*
> *The birds, like tender babies in your hands*
> *And the old men playing Chinese checkers by the trees*

Richard Harris sang the song first, but over one hundred artists have covered it in the years since, from Sinatra, to disco queen Donna Summer, to Waylon Jennings, whose version earned a him a Grammy. MacArthur Park is an actual park in the Westlake District of Los Angeles, site of composer Webb's picnic lunches with onetime sweetheart Suzy Horton, muse for at least four of his hit songs.

While juggling work in Los Angeles at Chianti and The Green House, along with family in San Francisco, Larry also began to bring to fruition Spectrum Foods' next venture, MacArthur Park Restaurant. He had a theme song and a muse. That was a good start.

Jerry was busy, too, with more than just the restaurants. Drawing on his early Joseph Magnin experience, he opened his own store, Jerry Magnin, on Rodeo Drive in Beverly Hills. It featured clothes by European designers. Shortly after, he teamed with Ralph Lauren to open Polo Ralph Lauren Beverly Hills, the first standalone Polo store.

As Larry said, there was no formal plan. For anything. No focus groups, no Survey Monkey. Most of the time he and Jerry went off gut feeling more than anything else.

Neither man considered how Spectrum Foods might benefit from Jerry's sartorial projects, but there turned out to be a wonderful synergy between them and the restaurants. A man might buy a beautiful suit from Jerry in the afternoon, then sit down to a perfect dinner at Chianti that night. The buzz grew louder.

As significant as Jerry's contributions were to Larry's early restaurant career, one playful, not quite "strictly business" moment dwarfed them all.

One morning in September of 1972 Jerry called Larry and asked, "Who knows you better than your own mother?"

Larry thought for a moment, and laughed. "You do, Jerry."

"That's right, me. I do. And last night I met your future wife. She came in to Chianti. She was with the actor David Ladd. I got her number. You've got to ask her out."

Larry was very busy at the time. MacArthur Park, his I'll-show-Mimi San Francisco restaurant, was opening October 10. Mimi may have provided significant inspiration for that restaurant, but as he accepted the reality of the situation, he had starting dating again. Soon he was " having a hell of a good time."

As the handsome, charismatic, young proprietor of one of the hottest restaurants in town, Larry was a very eligible bachelor. "Free love" was all the rage, and he wasn't in Toledo anymore. What was good for the goose also turned out to be very good for the gander. Larry had finally moved on.

Jerry suggested Larry invite his "future wife" to bucolic Ojai for the weekend. Jerry and his wife were already planning to go; Larry and his date were more than welcome to join them.

Larry phoned the prospect—at just twenty-five, she was ten years younger than Larry—and invited her to Ojai.

"Oh, that's very nice, but I'm sorry, no!" she replied. "Perhaps you could call for a dinner date sometime instead?"

After taking took her brushoff in stride and finding another date for the weekend, Larry called the woman again. She agreed to dinner. Once she had, Larry explained there was just one small hitch: he was flying down from San Francisco and his car was in the shop. Would she be able to meet him at the airport?

As Larry approached the yellow Mustang idling outside arrivals at LAX, he spotted his date behind the wheel and let out a sigh of relief. In this as in so many other matters, he and his business partner had what Jerry would later call "similar vision."

Larry introduced himself and offered the woman, Deborah Dudley, a choice: they could eat at The Green House or Chianti. She didn't hesitate.

"Chianti. The Green House is tacky."

She didn't know Larry owned both.

"Chianti, then," said Larry, smiling.

He lit her cigarette, and they headed for the restaurant. When she stopped for he gas, Larry paid for it—something no man had ever done before.

The dinner went well. They kept in touch after, each sensing potential. But both were busy at work: Larry with Spectrum—the soon-to-open MacArthur Park in particular—and Debby with her duties for the well-connected political consultant Don Solem.

Larry's ability to scout locations and negotiate favorable leases is a strength developed over decades as a restaurateur. Part of that resulted from a novice mistake: Larry and Jerry signed a five-year lease when they bought Chianti, something Larry eventually regretted, coming to prefer instead a twenty-year benchmark.

He picked an absolute winner for MacArthur Park: 607 Front Street in San Francisco, an old brick warehouse built on bay fill that years before had been part of the bustling Produce District. Thousands of potential customers worked in the nearby Financial District and in the advertising agencies, law firms, architectural offices, and antique shops that made up the neighborhood. Bordering North Beach and Chinatown, all three affiliates of the national television networks were there, too.

Alcoa-Perini developed the adjacent Golden Gateway Center in the 1960s, at the time the largest mixed-use urban residential complex in the country—1200 luxury units in four towers, all located over office, retail, and garage spaces. Mimi's father, Sonny, and brother, Mel, worked out of the Dean Witter office in one of the buildings.

For all the hustle and bustle, MacArthur Park's block, from Jackson to Pacific, was shaded and tranquil. The Golden Gateway development included the sculpture-filled Sydney Walton Square Park, a popular lunchtime gathering spot for brown baggers. Directly across from the restaurant, the park's perimeter berms buffered it from the surrounding streets, while curving concrete paths flowed through open expanses of lawn and small groves of trees, as though presaging the forest bathing trend that would follow years later.

Larry was determined to make MacArthur Park "dreamier than anything anyone had ever dreamed before." Mimi would have to take note. The hostesses would wear yellow dresses, as in Webb's song, though they wouldn't be uniforms. The women would be able to pick out their own dresses, as long as they were yellow. Keeping with the theme of the song, there would also be birds—live birds, which turned out to be peacocks housed in their own aviary. Peacock feathers became universal shorthand for West Coast hedonism and decadence, as described in the 1978 NBC News special report on Marin County, *I Want It All Now*.

Water flowed through clear acrylic tables from a central fountain via half-inch tubing—which worked well until the water eventually got scummy and clogged the tubes, ultimately exploding them.

The menu was 1970s hippie cuisine. "Whatever went well with dope," Larry once quipped.

Larry was excited to open in his adopted hometown. The stakes were high. Succeeding as he had in Los Angeles with Chianti was one thing; doing so—or *failing* to do so—in San Francisco before family and friends would be something else altogether. He and Jerry sent out special invitations to the October 10, 1972, opening: four-inch silver, stainless steel squares upon which was embossed:

> *each bud*
> *each flower*
> *each leaf*
> *each tree*
> *each touch*
> *each taste*
> *each friend*
> *We'd like to share a private opening of MacArthur Park with our friends. October 10, 1972. 8pm. 607 Front Street.*

Restaurants had not yet rolled out the "kid friendly" concept, but for three young San Franciscans—Michael, Laura, and Tony—MacArthur Park was often a very fun place. They felt pride of ownership from the start, contributing hours of child labor to the construction of a Tinkertoy-like wine rack that dominated the brick wall behind the bar. The kids spent so much time there that MacArthur Park—as well as Sydney Walton Square and the Golden Gateway complex—soon felt like a second home. The chef even placed a sandwich on the permanent menu for the notoriously finicky baby of the bunch: Tony's Tuna.

The restaurant got off to a promising start. It was large and open, "nice" but far from formal or stuffy. Columnist Jack Shelton wrote that it "looks like the kind of place (hip movie stars) Ali McGraw and Steve McQueen would have dinner to discuss their divorce." Scores, and eventually hundreds, of "beautiful people" began to gather there for happy hour. Especially on Friday nights, they were drawn by something simple, smart, and—at the time—rare: free appetizers like chips or crudités. It was nothing fancy, but it was free.

With MacArthur Park up and running, Larry now worked some days in San Francisco, some in Los Angeles. He and Debby were not yet exclusive, but they saw each other regularly, to the extent their busy schedules would allow.

A few months into their burgeoning back-and-forth, a new arrival appeared on the scene. Like Debby, he would turn out to play a key role in Larry's life, a trusted foxhole friend and confidant for the next fifty years.

First though, there was an addition to Spectrum's portfolio.

If The Green House was a little "more Jerry," and MacArthur Park "more Larry," Harry's Bar was a joint production that grew out of an inspirational trip to Italy. They knew that Chianti was thriving in great part because of their commitment to authentic contemporary Italian food, as opposed to the stock spaghetti-and-meatballs-type dishes most "Italian" restaurants in America served. They were determined to not merely maintain but deepen that commitment.

In Italy Larry and Jerry fell in love with Harry's Bar in Florence, returning several nights in a row. They got to know owner Enrico Mariotti and legendary barman Lio Vadorini. With Mariotti's full blessing, they returned to Los Angeles to create an exact replica of Harry's Bar. Mariotti even put them in touch with his furniture maker, so that the interiors would be precise matches. Larry and Jerry sent their architect to Florence, and he copied the restaurant to a tee.

Remarkably, there was no contract, no licensing agreement, no royalties expected. Enrico recognized brothers from another mother. He trusted the Californians to do it right and wanted nothing in return, just as his friend Giuseppe Cipriani had trusted him and his partner Raffaello Sabatini when they opened their Harry's in Florence in 1953.

Cipriani had opened the original Harry's in Venice in 1931, which quickly flourished, becoming "home" to European royalty as well as Americans like Katherine Hepburn, Humphrey Bogart, Joe DiMaggio, and Ernest Hemingway when they were in the City of Canals.

When Cipriani was a barman at the Hotel Europa in Venice, he lent 10,000 lira to Harry Pickering, a well-bred but struggling young American. Pickering stopped coming around shortly thereafter, and Cipriani assumed he'd never see the money again. Two years later, Pickering appeared out of nowhere, thanked Giuseppe and paid the debt. But that wasn't all.

"In gratitude, I'm adding another forty thousand lira, so that you can open a bar of your own for high society," he proclaimed. "I think they'll call it Harry's Bar. Not a bad name."

Evidently Cipriani hadn't forgotten his earlier good fortune when he heard that Mariotti and Sabatini wanted to open a Harry's in Florence. He didn't hoard trade secrets or try to extract a franchise fee as many might have; instead, he encouraged Enrico and Raffaello to "borrow" Harry's Venice mainstays (some say original creations), like carpaccio and the Bellini, a champagne and pureed-white-peach cocktail.

Larry, Jerry Magnin, and Chuck Frank

Nor did it appear that Mariotti had forgotten Cipriani's generosity nearly twenty years later when Larry and Jerry came around. It was natural for Enrico to pay it forward when he met the Californians, with whom he felt an immediate connection. One generous good turn sparked another: Cipriani to Pickering; Cipriani to Mariotti and Sabatini; Mariotti and Sabatini to Mindel and Magnin.

Enrico and Lio flew in for the Harry's Los Angeles 1972 opening. Lio spontaneously worked the bar that night, adding his own stamp of approval and authenticity. Harry's Bar Century City was no cheesy knockoff; Larry and Jerry had created a legitimate Harry's Bar in America.

Larry chatting with retired barman Lio Vadorini, who called in when he found out that Larry was dining at Harry's Bar in Florence; June 2023.

Years later, Lio looked after Larry's daughter Laura when she spent a semester in Florence. Harry's was her post office and bank. Later still, in June 2023, when Larry, Debby, and all five "kids" were eating at Harry's in Florence, their waiter brought a telephone to the table. Now-retired Lio had phoned in to welcome back his good friend "Lorenzo."

Larry and Jerry decided that Spectrum Foods could use a controller, someone who would take charge of the company's finances. One morning Jerry was conducting a phone interview with an out-of-state candidate. An older Joseph Magnin employee who happened to be in Jerry's Beverly Hills store overheard the conversation. Jerry knew the man, Marvin Frank—and he knew him well. Marvin was Jerry's brother Don's best friend. Marvin volunteered that his son, Chuck, might be the right man for the controller job.

Things moved quickly. Twenty-three-year-old Chuck Frank, a recent Wharton grad who had just passed his CPA exam, flew west from Pennsylvania. Larry picked him up at LAX in his Morgan, a stylish, if unreliable, British roadster.

When flying to San Francisco, value-conscious Larry often killed two birds with one stone: he would drop the frequently-in-need-of-service car at a shop close to the airport, allowing the mechanic several unrushed days to fix the problem. What's more, Larry got "free" airport parking out of the deal.

Larry and Chuck drove straight to Century City and Spectrum Foods' newest restaurant: Harry's Bar and American Grill.

Larry spent most of the night in the kitchen, calibrating the coffee machine.

"Remember, I was a coffee guy," Larry explained. "That was the only restaurant thing I knew more about than anyone else. I just tried to hire the best and let them do their thing."

Chuck loved Larry and Jerry's boldness and enthusiasm. Their somewhat informal controls and procedures gave him pause, however.

For almost three years, Spectrum—Chianti, The Green House, MacArthur Park, and Harry's Bar—had been a freewheeling, seat-of-the-pants operation, scrambling to stay afloat. As Chuck got a sense of the company's finances, he began to introduce new practices. If there were still thousands of dollars in uncounted cash atop their desks, for example, office workers were no longer permitted to walk out at 5:00 p.m. sharp. Chuck spent at least one night by himself in the office, shaking his head in disbelief while asking, *What are we doing?*

He learned that Spectrum was behind on monthly payments to more than forty vendors—meat, produce, wine, linens, and more. He met with each and gave his solemn word that Spectrum would eventually pay. Some agreed to wait three months to be paid in full, others up to thirty-six. He worked out an agreement with Norm Boyer, Spectrum's Union Bank man at the time, allowing for the occasional overdraft.

Things began to stabilize. The company stayed current on new bills and chipped away at old ones, never missing a payment. But even as Chuck and Larry vowed they would stand on their word and see Spectrum to the end—as opposed to quitting or declaring bankruptcy—they were still open to a sale. If a larger company with deeper pockets could see Spectrum's potential and wanted to swoop in, buy the company, trim whatever was necessary, and provide a well-funded fresh start, they would consider an offer. But after two unsuccessful years trying "to give Spectrum away," Larry, Jerry, and Chuck soldiered on.

Determined to cut nonessential costs, Chuck came to believe Spectrum could find cheaper office space for the company's executive and administrative staff, who were working out of fancy digs in the Mutual Benefits Life Insurance Tower on Wilshire. He took a long look at Chianti's liquor storeroom and realized that, with some reorganization, they could create room for a small office right there—including a playpen for Chuck's twin daughters. He bartered meals to movers, painters, and carpet installers, and soon Spectrum had a nice-enough "free" new office in space they were already leasing.

There was little to no margin for error. Each day Chuck's wife, Barbara, would deposit money in whichever of the twelve bank accounts was in most desperate need. Money didn't move with a computer keystroke then; it took days to clear. Sometimes—but not always—Tuesday or Wednesday brought a smidgen of relief, when the week's American Express money arrived. Walking such a sharp knife's edge was nerve-racking.

One day the Immigration and Naturalization Service (INS) raided a house where many of The Green House's busboys and kitchen staff lived. The men couldn't produce the required employment eligibility verification documents, so they could not work that day. Many were deported to Mexico and wandered back over the next two weeks. In the interim, Larry himself may have scrubbed a dish or two.

Larry and Chuck shared a secretary who sometimes got overwhelmed, fleeing to the bathroom to hyperventilate.

Very early one Sunday someone broke into Harry's and stole the two-thousand-pound safe containing both Friday and Saturday night's proceeds. Larry and Chuck suspected it was an inside job. Their insurance agent estimated it would take at least two months for the carrier to pay, a delay that would have had disastrous consequences for Spectrum. Amazingly, the next day the agent, Sy Aaronson, appeared and peeled off fifty one-hundred-dollar bills from his personal roll. He told Larry and Chuck to pay him back once corporate came through.

Authorities found the safe months later, pushed down a canyon above Los Angeles.

The restaurant business was full of characters, then even more than now. Many of Larry's current friends—warm and wonderful people—skew fairly conservative. Fifty years ago, though, Larry regularly interacted with some very colorful personalities who definitely could not be called conservative.

One evening he and Debby were eating at The Green House. Now that she knew Larry *owned* The Green House, Debby cheerfully consented to occasional dinners there, despite her first-date assessment that it was "tacky." She was a good sport.

Larry heard another diner say "MacArthur Park" several times.

His curiosity piqued and pride activated, he went over to the man's table.

"I couldn't help but hear you mention MacArthur Park," he began. "How do you know about MacArthur Park? That's my restaurant in San Francisco."

Puzzled, the man said, "MacArthur Park is my *song*. I wrote it. I don't know anything about any restaurant in San Francisco."

Larry had walked over to the man thinking he was trying to impress his date by exaggerating his relationship to Larry's hip new place. Larry intended to clear that up, but he softened when he learned that "MacArthur Park" was by all measures even more the diner's calling card than it was his own.

Songwriter Jimmy Webb and Larry ended up having a fun conversation, after which Larry sent a bottle of wine to his table. Larry told Webb's waiter to tell him that Mr. Mindel would like to offer a complimentary bottle of wine. Customarily, the appreciative diner selects a decent wine from the middle of the price list. Webb unabashedly ordered the most expensive bottle on the menu. Rock stars!

Larry and Webb crossed paths at Spectrum restaurants and around town several times after that, and Webb invited Larry and Debby to his July 1974 wedding. Although his own Campo de Encino party house had previously hosted the celebrated 1970 Los Angeles Philharmonic Nude Chamber Music Concerto, featuring a pregnant cellist, the wedding was not held there. Instead, Webb and his fiancée were married at his brother-in-law Jim Messina's Ojai ranch.

Webb married Patsy Sullivan, the seventeen-year-old daughter of screen actor Barry Sullivan and Swedish actress and model Gita Hall. Webb and Patsy met when they were photographed for the cover of *Teen Magazine* in 1968; he was twenty-two, she was twelve. They started dating a year later, and she gave birth to their first child when she was sixteen, a year and a half before the wedding.

The wedding was a classic 1970s entertainment industry event:

over 400 guests, including singers Joni Mitchell, Joe Cocker, Kenny Loggins, Ike Turner, and Johnny Rivers, as well as actors Beau Bridges and Lynda Carter. The bride arrived in the vintage Rolls Royce that James Dean used in the movie *Giant,* and a hot air balloon was tethered nearby in honor of the Fifth Dimension hit "Up, Up and Away," which Webb wrote. One female guest entered topless—maybe even naked—on horseback.

Debby enjoyed herself at the party, but, as a very down-to-earth young woman who had grown up in Beverly Hills, including going to school with stars' children, she was hard to dazzle. To this day Larry facetiously describes her as "an Irish washerwoman." He was more taken in by the spectacle than she.

The Webb wedding was a fun weekend away. But reality awaited Larry upon his return to Los Angeles. No matter what they tried with The Green House, it kept losing money.

Reluctantly, Larry, Jerry, and Chuck finally agreed to pull the plug. Larry worked hard to find a tenant to take over their Mutual Benefits Life Insurance tower lease. He was relieved to find another qualified restaurateur, a man with a track record and a vision. Adequately financed, he was eager to occupy the space. Spectrum was now free to wear the loss, learn their lessons, and move on.

Or so they believed. Not so fast, said the high-rise's property manager, San Francisco-based Shorenstein Corporation.

"We don't believe this fellow you've brought in to assume your lease is as qualified as you think. The restaurant business is no easy game. This new guy could very well go bust, and then where would we be? You signed a lease, we want you to honor it."

Jerry may have been disappointed that The Green House was struggling. Larry was devastated. It felt like life or death for him; this was no casual passion project. He could see whatever money he had made from the Caswell sale vanishing. How would he support his family? He was now back on the courts of his youth, fighting desperately

Lorenzo!

not to lose.

After several conversations, Larry and Jerry decided to ask their fathers for help—not a request they made lightly. Each was determined to make it on his own, but both also realized they would be fools not to utilize the help at hand for this particular situation.

It's unlikely that Larry and Jerry were negotiating with someone high up in the Shorenstein Company when trying to sell the Mutual Benefits Life tower lease—initial talks were almost assuredly with a subordinate. When the men realized that having the Magnin name on the lease gave the Shorenstein Corporation a sense of security it was not keen to relinquish, they asked Jerry's father, Cyril Magnin, as well as Larry's father, to fly in for their next landlord-tenant meeting.

Cyril was described in one *San Francisco Chronicle* story as an "iconic San Francisco businessman and philanthropist." Another called him a "legendary civic booster and bon vivant, San Francisco's first chief of protocol." There's a street named after him in downtown San Francisco, and—as became evident during the initial 5900 Wilshire dealings—he was close with Walter Shorenstein, head of the Shorenstein Corporation. Sy was still president of Chock full o'Nuts, so he, too, brought plenty of experience and presence to the matter.

Larry and Jerry took the lead in the meeting, explaining they had met the terms of the lease and should be allowed to leave. When the Shorenstein representative began to rebut their argument, Sy got angry, stood up, and declared that Shorenstein's position was not only unfair, but it was also illegal. By the time the meeting ended, Spectrum was free from their lease and free to close The Green House books. It was one of the best days of Larry's life, having a "father with clout," a father who, however dimly he originally viewed his son's decision to enter the restaurant business, nevertheless showed up for him when he needed his help.

Cyril and Sy offered valuable counsel and a different, perhaps more direct, form of help shortly after the Shorenstein liberation. When Jerry and Larry had decided to expand beyond Chianti, they needed more money, so they brought in outside investors, forming Spectrum Foods. Eventually some of these investors wanted a say in how the company was run.

"Jerry, you run the Los Angeles restaurants. Larry, you stay up in San Francisco, running MacArthur Park. There's no need for you to keep flying up and down," one investor insisted.

Larry did not like this.

"The restaurant business is one of the most individualistic there is. It's all about having and executing a personal vision," he later explained. "No way did I want someone telling me what to do."

To purchase their freedom and the autonomy they craved, Larry and Jerry would have to buy significant shares of the investors' stakes.

Larry had bought his share of Chianti on his own, using money from the Caswell sale. His father did not invest, since he believed it to be a risky, maybe even disreputable and foolish, proposition. But when it came time to buy out—or at least buy down—the outside investors, Sy, like Cyril, cut a check. The older men saw what their sons had done with Chianti and Harry's, and MacArthur Park looked promising. They could give Larry and Jerry a mulligan on The Green House; otherwise Spectrum Foods appeared to be a reasonable bet.

Larry and Jerry Magnin at MacArthur Park third anniversary party, 1975

The buyout was difficult. The investors were not eager to cede power, likely because they, too, sensed a real future for the company.

Larry gave "the presentation of his life" at one of the final negotiations, again taken by a sense of fighting desperately. When Larry disappeared after the meeting concluded successfully, Chuck went to look for him. He found him in the men's room, passed out on a toilet. No alcohol was involved. Larry had simply left it all on the field, given everything he had until his body called a temporary halt.

Although major challenges like getting out of The Green House lease and fending off ambitious investors often arose, business sometimes ran smoothly. Spectrum's mission was to provide great food and service in a nice environment at reasonable prices; it wasn't impossible. Eventually they amassed enough successful days that it was time for a party.

MacArthur Park turned three in the fall of 1975. The *Oakland Tribune* described the restaurant as "highly successful"; the *San Francisco Chronicle* said it was "thriving"; and the *California Post* described it as "one of San Francisco's most popular restaurants." Business was good.

In Larry's mind, good could always be better. He and Jerry worked with their press agent to come up with an idea to increase buzz: a third anniversary party in Webb's honor, with a planeload of Webb's celebrity pals from Los Angeles. Not one but two publications noted that a birthday party for a restaurant was out of the ordinary. The *San Francisco Chronicle* called the event "one of the season's most unusual parties—a birthday party for a restaurant." The *Vallejo Times* observed that "Most restaurants don't have birthdays. But MacArthur Park is not your average San Francisco restaurant, and co-owners Larry Mindel and Jerry Magnin do things with a flair."

The press agent did his job. In addition to the advance build-up, the party got plenty of follow-up coverage from the *San Francisco Chronicle, San Francisco Examiner,* and *Los Angeles Times.*

A priceless scrapbook was created to document the many stories and photos from the evening, offering a wonderful glimpse of the bygone '70s. From amusing hairstyles—had there been a "best hair" award, it definitely would have gone to singer Art Garfunkel—to fashions like mod Jerry's. Sporting long hair and a mustache, he wore aviator glasses, an ascot, and an open shirt collar resting on the wide lapels of a velvet blazer.

The *Los Angeles Times* reported that "the hosts at MacArthur Park were Jerry Magnin of Beverly Hills and Larry Mindel of San Francisco, who had his three beautiful children by his side." In the accompanying photos, daughter Laura was dressed in a fun, full-length peasant dress. A pink barrette pulled her wavy, brown hair back from her face, and the wine rack she and her brothers helped assemble was visible in the background. Son Tony—in need of a trim—sported a light-brown corduroy sports coat over a plaid shirt, along with checkered trousers. Larry wore a timeless, classic blue blazer with a blue button-down and an understated maroon tie. Michael followed his father's lead.

San Francisco Chronicle society columnist Pat Steger wrote, "As promised, the rock stars came out at night to celebrate the restaurant's third birthday with owners Larry Mindel and Jerry Magnin. Handsome Larry, who is separated from his wife Mimi (she was there), and dapper Jerry, who is separated from his wife, Erin (she wasn't), also operate that new 'in' place in LA, Harry's Bar and American Grill at the Century Plaza..." The rock stars in question included Art Garfunkel, Boz Scaggs, Kenny Loggins, Marilyn McCoo, Billy Davis Jr., Van Morrison, and Mickey Dolenz, lead singer of The Monkees.

Frank Sinatra, who admired Webb's songs and covered "By the Time I Get to Phoenix" on his 1968 *Cycles* album, calling it the greatest torch song ever, sent his regrets. A member of his staff represented him. Other no-shows included Kris Kristofferson, Rita Coolidge, Greg Allman and Cher, Alice Cooper, and Ringo Starr of the Beatles. (Laura would later swear she had been in a limo with Ringo, but most agree he was recording in London the night of the party.)

A wonderful photo shot from the side shows Larry shaking hands with actor Michael Douglas (*Wall Street, Fatal Attraction, The Kominsky Method*). Eye color aside, Douglas could play Larry convincingly; each man radiates a similar magnetism and intensity.

The special menu included Maine lobster plucked from the

restaurant's tanks, double-Frenched lamb chops, and lime mousse for dessert, a reference to "all the sweet, green icing flowing down" in the song after which the restaurant was named. There was a crystal-clear ice swan and a blue-tinted-ice flower basket.

Jerry's uncle, Walter Newman, looks on as Larry welcomes actor Michael Douglas (left) to MacArthur Park.

Larry and Jerry exchanged gifts with Jimmy Webb, who was there with his luminous wife Patsy—now of voting age! The restaurateurs presented Webb with a powder-blue crew neck sweater, specially knit to order by London's Mike Ross of Rivita. Webb gave Larry and Jerry the original conductor's score for "MacArthur Park."

The party went long. The *LA Times* wrote, "The party at MacArthur Park celebrating the restaurant's third birthday didn't end until

3:00 a.m. And even then some of the guests—like guest of honor Jimmy Webb, Art Garfunkel, Van Morrison and others—were still in a mood to party, so they drove across the bridge to Sausalito where they carried on at the Record Plant until 4:00 p.m. the following afternoon." This was before Red Bull!

Larry moved out of his house in Sausalito for several days, graciously turning it over to Webb and Garfunkel and their friends, a decision he later regarded with at least some ambivalence. They did a seventies rock star number on the house.

Overall though, MacArthur Park's third birthday party was a huge success, elevating the stature and profile of the already-flourishing restaurant. Larry and Jerry had a blast. They knew it was good for business; but, beyond that, they enjoyed throwing the party and had a sense that they might be pretty good at it.

In addition to the other media coverage, the MacArthur Park party appeared three times in Herb Caen's column, once as a "coming attraction" and later in two postmortems.

Today people can pick their news and commentary from a wide array of digital sources, from traditional news outlets to friends' social media to far-off TikTok influencers. Choices were far more limited in the 1970s. In San Francisco, "everybody"—from transplants to natives, hobos to heiresses, parking attendants to CEOs—read Herb Caen's daily column in the *San Francisco Chronicle*. Caen's popularity made possible a "common conversation" throughout Northern California. Being mentioned in his column was a real feather in most people's caps—even if some may have pretended otherwise.

Each column was a thousand-word collection of twenty-plus short items: local news, inside scoops, celebrity gossip, one-liners, offbeat anecdotes. Caen wrote for nearly sixty years, a remarkable 16,000 columns. He was a local columnist who achieved national prominence and a Pulitzer Prize, known as "the voice and conscience of his city." The day Caen died, President Bill Clinton issued a special statement, saying, "Surely no one knew better the vibrancy and eccentricities of The City, his city, San Francisco, than did Herb Caen."

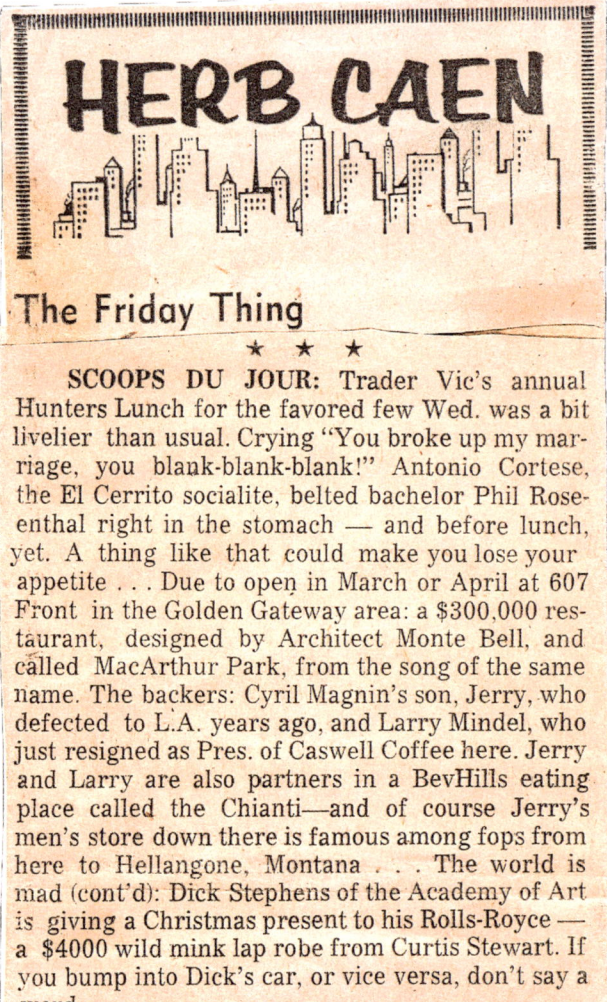

San Francisco Chronicle, December 3, 1971

Caen joked that he was an unlikely Pulitzer winner, because the prize is usually awarded to journalism that is "serious, heavy, deep—all the things I'm not." He often headed the last day of the workweek's column "Friday Fishwrap."

Two short weeks after he wrote a column disclosing he had inoperable lung cancer, the city designated a stretch of the Embarcadero to be renamed Herb Caen Way—unheard of celerity for the otherwise plodding bureaucracy. 75,000 people showed up for the dedication.

Caen often brought residents together in a fun, playful way. He once wrote, "A shopper was looking for a Barbie doll. 'Does Barbie come with Ken?' he asked the perky saleswoman. 'Actually, no,' she answered slyly. 'Barbie comes with G.I. Joe—she fakes it with Ken.'"

Not long after the Macarthur Park celebration, in February 1977, Larry and Jerry hosted another memorable party, this one a fortieth birthday for Chianti. The restaurant was over thirty years old and had a long history before Larry and Jerry revitalized it.

Like the MacArthur Park bash, the Chianti party was also memorialized in a scrapbook that came to rest on a shelf in Larry's office, a rich, reddish-brown leather portfolio with *Forty Happy Years: an Affectionate History of the Chianti* embossed in gold on the front. Honoring special guest Webb at the MacArthur Park party worked so well that Spectrum decided on a similar approach for Chianti, flying in founder Romeo Salta from New York.

Salta—born Romeo Saltamacchia—entered the United States as a penniless and illegal immigrant in 1929. A cabin boy on an Italian liner, he jumped ship, working restaurant and nightclub jobs in New York and the Midwest. Eventually settling in Los Angeles, he and a partner opened Chianti in 1937.

After he and his wife divorced, Salta returned to New York and opened Mercurio, followed by the eponymous and very successful Romeo Salta on West Fifty-Sixth.

"New York has never had an Italian restaurant as good as Romeo Salta was in its heyday," wrote Mimi Sheraton, *New York Times* restaurant critic, upon Salta's death in 1998.

Larry characterized Salta's appearance at the Chianti party as his "triumphant return" to Los Angeles. Salta beamed in every photograph, delighted to see his "baby" going strong once again and touched to be remembered and honored all those years later.

Jerry, founder Romeo Salta, and Larry toast Chianti's 40th anniversary, 1977.

Larry looked very sharp in a dark three-piece suit. Laura dressed for an Italian restaurant—her green blouse was dotted with Roman numerals. Several full-page black-and-white photos were published of Larry, Mimi, Michael, Laura, and Tony. In one, each looked in a different direction, Mona Lisa Mimi smiling inscrutably. This was six or seven years after the split, but everyone appeared to be getting along well. Mimi's sister-in-law Gayle Blum shared that Mimi often remarked, "I go where my kids go."

Other highlights included: a handwritten note from Larry's

mom, Ellie, wishing him good luck and expressing regrets that she and Sy couldn't attend ("Somehow Sy and I miss the great parties and endure the boring ones," she quipped); a thank-you and photos of John Tunney, the just-retired United States Senator and son of heavyweight champ Gene; and a yellow Western Union telegram from Larry's associates at MacArthur Park that read, "IF LEONARDO HAD CONCEIVED A RESTAURANT IT SURELY WOULD HAVE BEEN CALLED CHIANTI ENJOY ENJOY ENJOY."

Another telegram read, "UNA COSA ALA VOLTA (*one thing at a time*) CONGRATULATIONS ON A MUCH-DESERVED SUCCESS LOVE DEBBY."

Larry and Debby, 1978

A year and a half later, on the evening of October 20, 1978, Larry, Debby, and some of her friends had what was supposed to be a going-away dinner for Debby at Harry's Bar. She and Larry had been dating off and on for more than six years.

One nautical adventure typified the fun they had together. He had taken her out on the boat one afternoon, setting forth from Marina Del Rey. Frustrated when he couldn't find the harbor as they tried to return several hours later, he barked, "Goddamn it, Debby, where are we?"

"I have no idea."

"How can you not know? You *live* here!"

All the same, for whatever reason, Larry had not yet been able to pull the trigger. So, Debby had made the unilateral decision to fondly cut ties. She planned to move to New York the morning after.

Several Negronis into that emotional evening, Larry took a considerably more-sober Debby aside and told her, "I don't think you should move to New York."

"Oh really, that's nice," she replied. "What do you suggest I do instead?"

"I think we should get married."

She raised an eyebrow.

"I'm not joking. I'm serious.—I mean it. It took your leaving for me to realize how special you are. You're the perfect woman for me. I would be an absolute fool to let you go. Please. Let's get married."

This wasn't the Negronis talking. This was real for Larry. He had come to feel—with great gratitude—that Debby had "rescued" him over the past few years.

He was a self-described "mess" coming out of Mimi, struggling to play the sole-parent role so suddenly and unexpectedly thrust upon him. He treasured the fun love-connection spark he felt when he was with Debby, or talking on the phone, or writing her letters, as he often did. He also cherished beyond words her unselfish love for his children, how "she made us a family." Thirty-one-year-old Debby considered Larry's three young children a benefit not a cost.

By coincidence, Jerry and his wife, Lois, were in the restaurant that night.

"Tonight!" whooped Jerry when he heard about Larry's proposal, calling to charter a plane to Las Vegas. He was pleased to see his prediction play out that one day Deb would be Larry's wife.

Harry's general manager, Bill Moyles, emptied the register, filling two white-canvas bank bags with money. A charter could not be arranged, but soon a wedding party including Jerry, Moyles, and two of Debby's friends was on its way to LAX for the last commercial flight to Vegas. Not long after, the giddy group found itself at the Chapel of the Bells, the famous Las Vegas marriage mill, Rev. Eva Tubbs presiding.

Larry often said that Spectrum's early days were seat-of-the-pants. Everything more than worked out over time, though, so perhaps there's a lesson to be learned. Maybe spontaneity and "irrational" gut feeling aren't always the career and life risks conventional wisdom suggests. Double black diamond. Go big, or go home. No guts, no glory.

Not even the Sands, the Las Vegas casino in which Sonny, Larry's father-in-law, had an interest, would have extended any but the longest odds for bettors wagering on Larry and Debby. Forty-five years later the charming couple is still going strong.

Larry often calls Debby "the wind beneath my wings" and the "best thing that ever came out of Chianti." His grounded J.C. Penny-shopping bride (although some Larry-selected Armani did end up in her closet) didn't so much introduce him to a better set of values as she *reintroduced* him to his own Midwestern sense of right and wrong. Larry was relieved to "return home."

"Larry's a great guy. He's honest. He's empathetic, and he's so smart—even if he might not always be the easiest man to live with," Debby once commented with a smile.

Buoyed by the success of the Webb and Salta parties at MacArthur Park and Chianti, Larry and Jerry considered something similar for Harry's Bar. When they mentioned this to Los Angeles advertising executive Paul Keye, whose his firm created the famous "This is your brain on drugs" spot, he suggested something else.

Keye recalled that Nobel Prize-winner Ernest Hemingway mentioned the Venice Harry's repeatedly in his bestselling novel, *Across the River and into the Trees*:

> The waiter made the call while the Colonel was in the bathroom.
> "The Contessa is not at home, my Colonel," he said.
> "They believe you might find her at Harry's."
> "You find everything on earth at Harry's."
> "Yes, my Colonel. Except, perhaps, happiness."
> "I'll damn well find happiness too," the Colonel answered him.
> "Happiness, as you know, is a moveable feast."

Musing on this, Keye came up with an idea for a contest: the International Imitation Hemingway Competition. He bought ad space in *The New Yorker* and made a call for entries, which stated, "One very good page of very bad Hemingway will send you and a friend to Italy for dinner." The contest had two rules: entries had to mention Harry's Bar & Grill, and they had to be funny.

To everyone's delight and surprise, the contest turned out to be a real hit, drawing more than 24,000 entries and far more media attention in its first ten years than anyone ever anticipated. It even spawned not one but two anthologies, *The Best of Bad Hemingway, Volumes I and II*.

Television crews from as far away as Germany crowded into Harry's to film the judging, which over the years included novelist Ray Bradbury (*Fahrenheit 451, The Martian Chronicles*); Barnaby Conrad, bullfighting aficionado, novelist (*Matador*), and founder of the Santa Barbara Writers Conference; novelist Joseph Wambaugh (*The Onion Field, The Choirboys*); Los Angeles newspaper columnists Jack Smith and Digby Diehl; San Francisco poet and City Lights bookstore owner Lawrence Ferlinghetti; Herb Caen; and *Paris Review* founder and editor and participative journalist George Plimpton (*Paper Lion: Confessions of a Last-String Quarterback*).

Harry's in Century City was located in the ABC Entertainment Center, right across from the Century Plaza Hotel. In addition to hosting Grammy and Emmy awards shows, during the Reagan presidency it was also known as the "Western White House," given how often was he in residence. Laura and her brothers ran around the Entertainment Center, a mid-century outdoor plaza home not just to Harry's but to the Playboy Club, the Plitt Theater cinema, and the Shubert Theater, which hosted live stage productions. The Center was demolished in 2003, replaced by a modern building home to the Creative Artists Agency, which represents athletes like Joe Burrow and Nick Bosa, actor Tom Hanks, director Steven Spielberg, and many other A-listers.

Full Spectrum

Shortly before Larry and Debby tied the knot, Spectrum opened its second San Francisco restaurant, Ciao, located on Jackson Street at Front, just around the corner from MacArthur Park—a space occupied today by Kokkari.

Ciao was hip and packed from the start—customers loved it. MacArthur Park might have been a little goofy early on, a spot of its times; but Ciao had cutting-edge, contemporary Italian food and interior design. It gave customers the impression of being magically transported for the night to a very happening Milanese trattoria.

The restaurant was all white—right down to its original floor—and brightly lit with lots of chrome and mirrored surfaces. A Piaggio "Ciao" moped hung whimsically on one wall, its red taillight flashing.

Larry first saw the floor in Italy—squares of dimpled white rubber made by Pirelli, the performance automotive tire company. It was very sophisticated, but careless diners would drop their cigarette butts to the ground before grinding them out. The floor soon looked as though it had measles. Spectrum had to replace it in its entirety after just a few weeks with dark-grey, almost black, flooring that did not show the ash splotches. Doing so was not inexpensive.

Ciao was lauded for its exhibition pasta-making station, one of the nation's first. The *pastaio* (pasta maker) would roll out the from-scratch dough on a long table adjacent to customers, then hang cut fettuccini or linguini to dry on wooden dowels. Diners loved this extra bit of authenticity, but initially it wasn't done for show. The restaurant was so small, there simply wasn't room anywhere else for the station.

Larry and his associates at all the restaurants have always been superb marketing people, but the quality of what they sell has indisputably come first. When Spectrum decided to use a typeface that resembled lipstick for the Ciao logo, they were hardly putting lipstick on a pig. Confident and sexy is as confident and sexy does, and Ciao was both.

Imagery taken from noted Northern California artist Wayne Thiebaud's *Timaballo di riso*.

Larry later claimed that, in a fit of inspiration one night in a New York hotel, he grabbed Debby's lipstick and wrote "Ciao" on a napkin, creating the logo. Others remember it differently, as the product of a long and vinous stag "research" dinner one night in Italy. At the end of the evening, a waitress may have expressed her appreciation for the Spectrum guys by writing "Ciao" in lipstick on a napkin, perhaps including a number or an address? Maybe not. Who can remember all these years later?

Larry has always been known for his attention to detail. It's part of what makes him so good at what he does. He notices *everything* in his restaurants: if a light is too bright, or not bright enough; whether music is too loud or too soft. He sees and hears it, ensuring it be made right—occasionally to daughter Laura's consternation, who would plead, "Can't we just have dinner, Dad?"

In one instance, Larry's obsession with detail led to a significant series of relationships and chain of events.

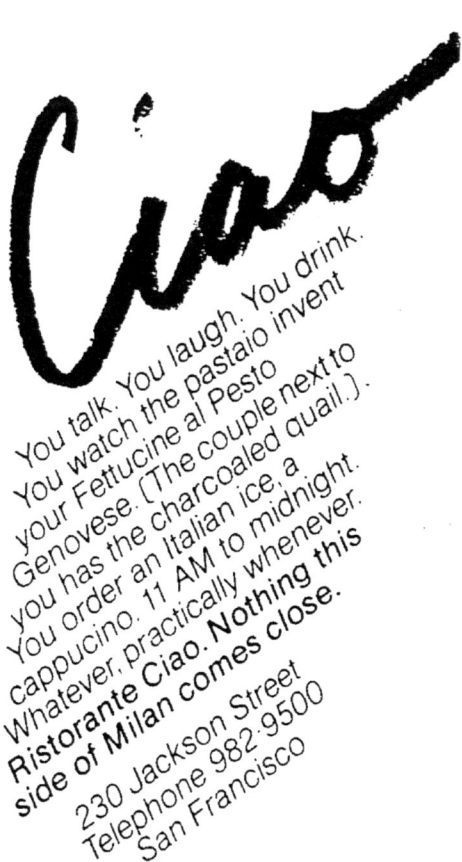

Ciao

You talk. You laugh. You drink. You watch the pastaio invent your Fettucine al Pesto Genovese. (The couple next to you has the charcoaled quail.). You order an Italian ice, a cappucino. 11 AM to midnight. Whatever, practically whenever. Ristorante Ciao. Nothing comes close. side of Milan 230 Jackson Street Telephone 982-9500 San Francisco

In the late seventies his office was located on the waterfront at Pier 1, just north of the Ferry Building, across from Justin Herman Plaza and the Hyatt Regency Hotel. Like other tenants, Larry parked his car in the pier's cavernous two-story, stucco bulkhead building.

The office was unique. In a 1981 interview, Larry told the *San Francisco Examiner* that he "wouldn't give it up for the world. I was looking for an office that would be within walking distance of MacArthur Park and Ciao. The places I found were either too big or too expensive. When I followed up on an ad in the newspaper, the man on the phone told me it had no toilet facilities, no heat, and was 100 feet long but only 10 feet wide. I was about to hang up, when he added that it was on the water and had a gangplank. I was sold right there."

The entrance to the Spectrum office was a gangplank—a moveable bridge from ship to shore—which came from an old Alaskan steamer. Larry had mirrors set into the walls opposite the 100 or so small windows that looked out on the bay, making the space feel bigger. There was no built-in heat—one winter the ball on executive assistant Valerie Stannard's IBM electric typewriter froze—and no bathroom either, save the old longshoreman's toilet at the end of the pier. Larry installed portable electric water heaters and, he explained, "for a bathroom emergency I brought in a marine chemical toilet, which no one has ever had to use; the longshoreman's lav works just fine."

Larry often parked next to a red 1972 Alfa Romeo GTV sporting the personalized license plate CYNAR. He assumed that the owner had something to do with the importation or sale of Cynar (pronounced CHEE-nar), an Italian liqueur, or *digestivo*, something Europeans drink before or after a meal to aid digestion. Distinctive glass Cynar ashtrays sat atop restaurant tables all over Italy. Detail man Larry thought those same ashtrays would be a fun, authentic touch for soon-to-open Ciao. One day he left a note on the Alfa, asking if the owner could supply him with some.

Romano Chietti read the note and walked up the gangplank into the Spectrum office.

"I can get you the ashtrays," he announced.

Chietti was the West Coast Cynar importer. To this day he remains Cynar's number one booster, asserting that its primary ingredient, artichoke, makes Cynar the ideal "health drink." "Nothing filters the liver better," he says. "Campari you can only drink before lunch or dinner, but Cynar you can and *should* drink all day long!"

Romano represented Cynar, but he was also starting his own wine importation business. Before leasing a warehouse in the Bayview, he had crammed 300 cases of Pinot Grigio and Chianti Classico Reserva into his Marina District garage. Coincidentally, Romano lived very close to Mimi's house.

Romano claimed to be the first West Coast importer to bring in Pinot Grigio and Chianti Classico Reserva. He also helped introduce and popularize Brunello and Amarone. When he first got the warehouse, he worked from 8:00 a.m. to 8:00 p.m., unloading 1000 cases of Amarone from a shipping container—by himself.

At first Larry and Romano talked about the ashtrays. Soon the conversation turned to Ciao, and each recognized in the other a common spirit. It wasn't long before Romano began to play a key, if slightly unsung, role at Ciao. He became not just the restaurant's wine supplier, but its wine coach, too, educating the staff.

By Romano's estimates, in those days the typical wine list for an Italian restaurant in California featured 85 percent French wines, 10 percent California wines, and 5 percent mediocre Italian wines. At Ciao, he saw an opportunity to introduce diners to excellent—and affordable—Italian wines that complemented the dishes.

Working with his old acquaintance Franco Galli, whose official title at Spectrum was *maestro*—which meant he was in charge of food—Romano would taste every item on the menu and ask, "What Italian wine would go best with *this* dish?"

Five years of culinary school in his native Italy distinguished Romano from most other wine salesmen; unlike them, he understood the overall food-and-wine experience. Two or three times a week Romano and Franco would lead Ciao's staff through tastings that paired dishes with wines. Informed waiters and bartenders could then take what they learned and guide customers to satisfying wine selections.

Franco also grew up in Italy. He, too, went to culinary school there before signing on with Costa Cruises, known for its luxury ships. He and Romano would speculate about what Ciao and any other restaurants that followed could be "if Larry had the will" to make them authentically Italian—the cooks, the food, the waiters, everything. They saw that Larry "got it," and that a truly Italian spirit animated this nice Latvian boy from Toledo. But they also knew it would be a bold, trailblazing move on his part. Success was not guaranteed. They wondered: *did he have the will to make it happen?*

The notoriously clannish Italians recognized something in Larry and began to give him their provisional imprimatur. They hoped he could pull it off.

Larry has never been one to rest on his laurels. Even as Ciao was prospering, he began to feel that his beloved, offbeat MacArthur Park might need to change with the times, just as the nation was moving from Carter to Reagan. The restaurant had long ago outgrown its origin story—*let me show Mimi just how groovy I can be*—which faded as time passed and Larry married Debby, his "one-in-a-million." Now the mission was more traditional: he wanted the restaurant to regain its initial relevance and grow more profitable.

As Larry's inchoate feelings about MacArthur Park were coalescing into thoughts he could articulate and act upon, Jerry met a hospitality professional who had just moved to San Francisco from Chicago. Jerry suggested the young man meet with Larry.

Three historically brutal Chicago winters in a row—1976, 1977, and 1978—had prompted Bill Higgins to quit his dream job, pack his car, and head for San Francisco. He had neither employment nor housing lined up in advance, fairly common practice at that simpler—and cheaper—time.

Precocious, twenty-nine-year-old Higgins was one of six original partners in Chicago's whimsically named but extremely successful Lettuce Entertain You restaurant group, before working as general manager of the legendary Pump Room in the Ambassador East Hotel. The restaurant appeared in movies, including *North By Northwest*, *My Bodyguard*, and *Running Scared*, and variations of popular songs, such as Judy Garland's "Chicago (That Toddlin' Town)" and Sinatra's "My Kind of Town (Chicago Is)." Guests included Marilyn Monroe,

Elizabeth Taylor, Paul Newman, Ronald Reagan, John Belushi, Eddie Murphy, and Mick Jagger. After an incident at the Pump Room, Phil Collins was inspired to name his 1985 multi-platinum album *No Jacket Required*. It was definitely a place.

Bill had always had California in his sights. Growing up, he visited his grandparents in Atherton, and he loved the whole California scene, just as state-struck Larry had loved it when he arrived from the Midwest in 1960. There was a Bay Area "food revolution" going on that he and his Chicago restaurant buddy and fellow sunseeker Bill Upson wanted to experience.

"Alice Waters at Chez Panisse. Judy Rodgers and Jeremiah Tower there, too, before eventually opening Zuni and Stars, respectively. Patty Unterman with Hayes Street Grill. There was nothing like that in Chicago. We wanted to be a part of it," he later recalled.

"The two Bills," as they came to be known, went to San Francisco. When he arrived, Higgins met with James Nassikas, general manager of the Stanford Court Hotel. He didn't know Nassikas personally, but someone at the Ambassador East made the introduction. Nassikas met with Higgins and then sent him to Jerry, who sent him to Larry.

The two hit it off, and Larry began to think out loud, sharing with Bill his sense that MacArthur Park needed to change.

"The wheels were definitely already turning for Larry before we met," Higgins explained. "He was way ahead of the game. MacArthur Park was dated, if not dying, and Larry knew it. He was thinking maybe of turning it into a rib joint. I told him Upson and I were from Chicago. We knew ribs like the back of our hand. We could do that, no problem."

Larry hired Higgins as MacArthur Park's new general manager. Higgins brought in Upson as chef. All three agreed to significant changes. They would tighten the restaurant's focus, making it simpler and more straightforward—ribs, chicken, and fish—and more Midwestern. Perhaps it was another manifestation of Debby inspiring Larry to return to his "true self."

"The Bills," Larry, and Chuck Frank flew to Chicago and toured several packing houses. They ate at all ten restaurants featured in *Chicago* magazine's "Best Ribs" issue, before finally settling on the United American Meat Company as their sole supplier of baby back ribs. They built a smoker at the restaurant and installed a large grill.

They also changed MacArthur Park's look. It was still going to be the same high-ceilinged, old-brick-walled winner it had always been, but they got rid of the peacocks and exploding waterworks. They hung *Paris Review* art on the walls and leveraged Jerry's Ralph Lauren connection, outfitting the waiters in classic khaki trousers and blue oxford cloth shirts.

The Hal Riney and Partners advertising agency helped with the transformation, rolling out a new campaign with the slogan, "Best ribs in the city. Honest." Even the matchbooks were updated to feature the restaurant's name foregrounding a warm silhouette of the San Francisco skyline at sunset.

The updated MacArthur Park became one of the first restaurants to offer private label wines, a Spectrum cabernet and a Spectrum chardonnay from Charles Krug and Mondavi. Customers loved them, as did Spectrum—they were very profitable.

Upson sent a plane ticket to their old Pump House colleague Cindy Pawlcyn, who was visiting her parents in Minnesota. He included the message: "Congratulations, you're our new sous-chef."

Cindy didn't recall applying for the job. All the same, by November of 1979 she was ensconced in the kitchen at 607 Front.

"You open, I'll close," Upson told her.

Cindy had to be in by 6:30 a.m. to meet the fish sellers. The menu and restaurant as a whole became more fun and vibrant, retaining old favorites like Judy's Mud Pie, while adding new staples like a Cobb salad, potato skins, and onion strings.

Upson and Cindy worked hard in the kitchen, giving Higgins the thousand-yard stare, their chef's whites stained a permanent BBQ-sauce brown while he was out front, looking sharp, chatting up people, sipping the occasional glass of wine.

The makeover reinvigorated the restaurant. It was no longer just a pleasant, if somewhat eclectic, stop on a boulevardier's rounds. It was now *a real place*—delicious, familiar food conceived and prepared with just enough of a twist; attentive, professional service; a comfortable—grownup but not stuffy—vibe; reasonable prices. Smart, beautiful, fun-loving diners and drinkers flocked to the establishment.

Higgins met many of San Francisco's leading businesspeople, including the Pacific Union real estate development team. He had a passing acquaintance with its three founders: Bill Harlan, John Montgomery, and Peter Stocker. He knew more closely the man one level below them, Peter Palmisano.

Palmisano told Higgins that he and Upson ought to come check out Pacific Union's newest acquisition, the almost ramshackle Meadowood Resort in Napa. He wanted the Bills' take on it.

When they toured the property with Palmisano, the Bills realized he was looking for a chef and maybe even a general manager. Neither wanted to leave what they had just started at MacArthur Park, and neither was ready to live in the country. They wondered if it might be a fit for Cindy.

Somewhat reluctantly—they did not want to lose such a valuable co-worker—they mentioned the opportunity to her. After some deep thought about quality of life, Cindy decided to make the move.

Although she had been with Spectrum for less than a year, Larry had grown fond of Cindy. He wanted to throw her a going-away party.

"It was at his house. He opened his home for me," Cindy later recalled. "No one had ever done that before. Such a sweet guy."

Twenty-four-year-old Cindy worked magic at Meadowood and built a real name for herself. Three years later, in 1983, she felt confident enough to go out on her own, opening Mustards Grill in Napa. She invited Higgins and Upson to join her, and they accepted. Although the Pump Roomers were only with Spectrum for a little more than a thousand days, they made a huge contribution to the company.

It's not surprising that Real Restaurants, the company Higgins, Pawlcyn, and Upson formed when they opened Mustards, was such a success. Their establishments went on to include Bar Bocce, Bix, Bungalow 44, Buckeye Roadhouse, Corner Bar, Floodwater, Fog City, Picco, Playa, and Tra Vigne. An admitted stretch perhaps, but there seemed to be at least a hint of the old MacArthur Park spirit in all.

In a 2011 *Marin Independent Journal* interview, Higgins said, "Playfulness is important. Hey, it's fun. People want to have a good time when they go out. Whenever you can invoke or inject a little humor, it makes people more comfortable, more relaxed, happier."

MacArthur Park did so well that in 1981 Spectrum elected to open another one in Palo Alto. Larry found yet another ideal location: California Historical Landmark No. 895, originally a World War I recreation facility for troops training nearby, designed by the renowned architect Julia Morgan. MacArthur Park Palo Alto's interior features Morgan's signature exposed functional trusses. The restaurant is alive and well today.

For the opening, Larry's 200 invited guests met at MacArthur Park in the city. They hydrated; boarded buses to Townsend Street, across from today's Oracle Park, home of the Giants; and then traveled by private train to Palo Alto, hydrating more along the way. In Palo Alto they were met at the station—directly across from the new restaurant—and piped into the restaurant by the Stanford marching band.

Larry knows how to host a party.

Open to It

In 1980, after his restaurant in Eugene, Oregon didn't make it, Doug Biederbeck moved to San Francisco. Ed Moose hired him to work the door at the Washington Square Bar and Grill. Although working the door at the Square wasn't exactly the same as running the Pump Room, as Higgins had, it was a similar mark of distinction for a young hospitality man. It showed that someone with the power to hire and fire saw something special in him.

Doug didn't feel all that special Easter morning of 1981. He felt poor and a little left out. Moose had shut the restaurant for a week, taking the Square's famous softball team, Les Lapins Sauvages, on a tour of England and Ireland.

A good restaurant had *a famous softball team* and was known for its *penny pitching contests*? *Sports Illustrated* writer Ron Fimrite's *The Square* tells the story beautifully. The team was sort of tongue-in-cheek. Herb Caen, who called it the Washbag in his columns, played first base.

But the Square itself was no joke. For some people it was *the* place in San Francisco. Being known and accepted there conferred a warm feeling of arrival or belonging.

Since Doug didn't make that trip and was short on money, he asked the owner if there was anything he could do to make a few dollars during the restaurant's furlough.

Easter morning he was painting parts of the interior when the phone rang. A man asked for Moose. Doug replied that Moose was out of town. Being so affable, however—a born host—Doug talked with the caller for a bit. Soon enough the man, a headhunter, revealed that he wanted to get a recommendation from Moose, wondering if he knew of anyone in management who could help open a new Italian place on Union Street. "I'd like the job," Doug said. The man suggested he send a resume.

Sending a resume was not the simple keystroke then that it is today. First off, Doug had to write one. Restaurant people didn't have resumes in 1981; they showed up and talked with potential employers. Next he had to find an envelope and a stamp and put the resume in a mailbox. It took time for the resume to arrive at its destination and make its way to the recipient.

In their prime: Larry, Bill Moyles, Doug Biederbeck, Mark Walker, Franco Galli, Bill Upson, Bill Higgins

Shortly after sending his resume, Doug got a call from Bill Higgins, who had recently been promoted from MacArthur Park general manager to Spectrum's director of operations, overseeing all Spectrum restaurants: Chianti, Harry's, both MacArthur Parks, and Ciao. The two clicked immediately, and Higgins impulsively said, "Hey, I'm at the location now, going over some of the build-out. Can you meet me here in a few?"

Thinking quickly, Doug asked a co-worker to cover for him at the

Square, ducked out, and hopped on a 41 Union Muni bus.

By the time Higgins finished showing Doug around what would soon be Spectrum's sixth restaurant, he knew he wanted him as Prego's assistant general manager. Doug gave notice to Moose and began to train at Ciao, as the Prego construction corps finished their work.

Prego was an immediate smash—and so was Doug, quickly promoted from assistant to full general manager. Prego didn't take reservations and permitted no food substitutions. When asked why much later, a slightly abashed Doug shrugged, "because we could (get away with it)." That just fueled the restaurant's popularity. On Friday nights, diners would wait at the bar for a table for two, sometimes three, hours.

Part of Prego's appeal was its wood-fired, brick pizza oven. The idea was new at the time. Tommaso's in North Beach and the café at Chez Panisse in Berkeley were the only other restaurants built around such a feature. Bumps Baldauf, who built the Chez Panisse oven, fabricated Prego's as well. Far from hidden away in a back kitchen, the oven, like Ciao's pasta-making station, was out in the open, a central part of Prego, its true hearth, a visual and olfactory touchstone.

Wolfgang Puck ate at Prego when he was envisioning Spago, the hugely successful restaurant he would later create in Los Angeles. He liked the pizza idea so much that he "stole" Ed LaDou, Prego's primary pizza chef. Later, LaDou helped found California Pizza Kitchen. When Larry ate at Spago for the first time and saw an odd turn in the pizza oven's flue—a turn that Bumps *had* to design at Prego to accommodate an existing beam—it was clear to him that someone at Spago had replicated the Prego setup exactly, bend for bend, without understanding why the Prego vent was designed and executed as it was.

Shortly after Prego opened, Doug called his Eugene friend and colleague, Stanley Morris, explaining, "I got into a great situation down here, but I need some help. We just opened, and it's crazy busy. I need someone I know and trust, someone strong. You want a job?"

Stanley knew Doug from Eugene's Excelsior Café, where they both started in the restaurant business. The Excelsior was the Chez Panisse of the Northwest, founded by Stephanie Pearl Kimmel. Doug's call came at a key moment: Stanley was just about to leave for Cornell University's noted hotel and hospitality graduate school. Doug's offer piqued his interest, however, so Stanley flew to San Francisco in early

September 1981.

As soon as he walked into the restaurant, he knew he wanted the job. He would later explain that he had "no idea what food was then. I was way out of my depth. Prego was sexy. Larry wanted it to feel exciting, modern, and entertaining. There were handsome men and beautiful women serving equally attractive customers. The lighting made people look good—the lights were from Milan, they weren't Underwriters Laboratory approved at that point, but who cared? They made people look their best. There was special Donald Kaufman paint and original art on the walls. Jerry Magnin got Ralph Lauren to provide special grey flannel for the banquettes. Larry cared about place. I felt it as soon as I walked in."

Stanley had lunch with Larry, Doug, Bill, Franco, and executive chef Claudio Marchesan. After they finished eating, the Spectrum men said they would discuss amongst themselves a possible position for him and let him know before his evening flight back to Portland. They invited him to wait in the restaurant. He waited for some time. Finally, Higgins appeared and said, "Larry got wrapped up in something else, so we have to wait for him to make it official, but basically it comes down to one of two choices: you can pay to go to Cornell to get an education in hospitality management, or you can come here and we'll pay you for an even better education."

Eventually Larry reappeared. He apologized for the delay, saying that it had taken a while for him to check Stanley's references.

"*You* checked my references?" Stanley asked, surprised. This was his first brush with Larry the detail man, Larry who didn't delegate.

"Of course I did," Larry replied, as though it was the most logical thing in the world. "You start in a week."

As Larry walked to his car, he looked back and added, "I don't know exactly what it is about you, Stanley, but I have a feeling we're going to do some great things together."

Doug had been with Spectrum just six months longer than Stanley, but even that brief span was more than time enough to begin to know the boss's mania for detail. One night it was the chopped salad, which needed more lemon (Larry could never have enough lemon). Another busy night the issue was Doug's priorities.

When Larry arrived, he asked Doug, "How's the food tonight?"

Doug, who was greeting and seating customers, orchestrating staff, doing his best to create some semblance of order out of sheer chaos, gave him a quick, "I don't know, it's so busy I haven't had time to check." What he meant was *excellent as usual I'm sure, good to see you, we are really rocking, I'll swing by your table for a less hectic conversation once we get through this rush*. But that's not what he said. Instead, he kept working.

The next day Doug received a *letter* from Larry, explaining why that had been the wrong response to his inquiry. It wasn't a power play, so much as a reminder that food was of vital importance. All the great service, ambience, and reasonable pricing in the world meant nothing if the food wasn't up to Spectrum's high standards. A general manager should never forget this, not even when caught up in a temporary frenzy—however profitable that frenzy might be—as Doug had been that night.

Larry could have discussed this with Doug later that night when things calmed down. He could have called him the next day. But he chose to write, believing a letter would emphasize the importance of his point more powerfully than a conversation. And he was right: Doug still remembers the exchange forty years later.

Another incident saw Larry come within a carpaccio slice of firing Doug for immature behavior (the lines between work and pleasure blurred more often in 1982 than they do today). In fact, Larry *did* fire him, but Doug pleaded for a second chance, which Larry granted—to San Francisco's lasting benefit. Doug's fabulously successful Bix restaurant has been a Jackson Square institution for thirty-five years, extremely uncommon staying power in a notoriously fickle industry. The history between the two men makes Larry's annual holiday dinner at Bix with his sons all the more meaningful.

Doug's second chance didn't come without obligations. Larry sent him to run Prego Beverly Hills when Spectrum opened there in 1983. Doug was not keen to go, but he didn't have much choice given his near termination. Fortunately, Prego Beverly Hills prospered, and Doug ended up having a positive experience in the southland.

When Doug left for Beverly Hills, Stanley became Prego San Francisco's new general manager. He and Larry got closer as a result. Larry took Stanley out into the middle of Union Street, facing the restaurant, and told him, "You need to own everything from the middle of this street, this yellow line, into the door. This is your space. If it's dirty, sweep or hose it. If a light is out, change it. Don't depend on public works. Own it."

Stanley was in his late twenties, Larry in his mid-forties. It wasn't quite father-son, but Stanley would retain a deep, longstanding gratitude and respect for Larry, as well as for his mentorship.

"It was a young industry, and he groomed us to have his sensibilities. He liked visual people. He taught us that if a restaurant truly looks and feels right, is clear on the concept and consistent with food and service, the customer will feel comfortable spending his money. Larry believed that it all sets up *before* the transaction. Control what you can—the spaces, colors, lighting."

Stanley married young and divorced a handful of years later. At Prego, he had initiated what he thought was a discreet relationship with one of his male employees. Larry, the detail man who always seemed to see and know all, addressed the situation directly when he transferred the waiter from Prego to Ciao.

"I had to do it, Stanley. Randy works for you, and you're sleeping with him. Having a relationship with one of your employees only creates mistrust with the rest of your staff. And you need to come out at work. You're a great guy. Don't hide. Live your life."

"Larry was a very generous employer," Stanley recollected. "He shared profits, time, and knowledge. Beyond that though, Larry was very present, he helped a lot of people get through a lot of life. He had hundreds of employees, and he knew them all by name. Many leaders *say* their door is always open, but his truly was; he lived it. Some of us, our lives were messy. He didn't have to get involved, but he did. And he did it for me in a way that felt authentic, that made me feel special and seen. It was a huge turning point for me. I was twenty-eight, and this was a forty-six-year-old straight man telling me I was okay."

Stanley admired and appreciated Larry greatly, and he was quick to praise the restaurateur's drive and attention to detail. He also held in high regard Larry's aesthetic sensibility. Citing Ciao and Prego, Stanley also believed Larry's intuition helped set trends.

"It's not luck. He anticipates things. He is there waiting."

Bill Higgins essentially said the same when he declared that Larry was "way ahead of the game" when he felt the original MacArthur Park fading from relevance and knew that change was necessary.

What really set him apart according to Stanley—most likely remembering how Larry encouraged him to come out at work—was his empathy, his willingness to be right there alongside his associates as they hacked their way out of whatever thicket they were ensnared in.

When once asked if he had any words of wisdom for his descendants, Larry said, "Empathy. That's really the most important thing. Good guys do win, and part of being a good guy is being sincerely empathetic. Pay attention to the next person; your life will be better for it. When someone's hurting, feel that hurt yourself. Most of us have been hurt or will be hurt. Feel for other people."

Most see Larry as a winner, and he has won plenty, professionally and personally alike. But he has lost a lot as well in both arenas, and he remembers what those losses felt like. So, he tries to treat people kindly, because "you just never know what someone else is going through on a particular day." A lifetime of experience distilled into some very valuable wisdom.

When Stanley became Prego's general manager, he immediately suggested that Spectrum hire his and Doug's old friend, Marsha Guerrero, as assistant manager.

Marsha flew down from Eugene to interview with a very intimidating group she subsequently called "the Rolexes": Larry, Chuck, Franco, and Claudio, each sporting the pricey timepiece. Even though the men were not that much older than she, thirty-eight-year-old Marsha felt as though they were the "grown-ups." They asked challenging questions—especially Franco, who wanted her to understand that food would be his and Claudio's domain, not hers.

She got the job.

"I was thrilled. I was now working at Prego. The restaurant was so good. The food was outrageous. I didn't know how they did it, food that good with so many customers. And the waiters: a very glamorous and interesting cast of characters—there wasn't a formal waiting list for jobs at Prego, but the same people would call week after week and ask, 'you got any openings?' They really wanted to work there."

Like Stanley, Marsha noted Larry's visual sensibility.

"He was a *huge* influence on me and many others, too. It was so much more than just working in a restaurant. He changed the way I looked at things and experienced beauty—he really did. He's a businessman first, but he's also an artist."

Like he did with Stanley, Larry spoke directly to Marsha.

"He did not delegate. He did his own dirty work. I was absolutely *mortified* when he called me out, but I respected him for doing it himself rather than dumping it onto someone else, which he easily could have—maybe *should* have. I respected him, and I appreciated him for that, too, once I got over the embarrassment. He didn't have to involve himself in my personal life like that. I didn't have to be his mess, but he made it his concern, and that told me he cared about me."

Apparently love was in the air at Prego. Also like Stanley, Marsha was sleeping with a co-worker, Bobby, the chef who replaced Claudio when he departed to open Beverly Hills with Doug. Larry transferred her to MacArthur Park.

"It felt like a total demotion," she recalled. "We thought the people at MacArthur Park were a bunch of goody-two-shoes all-Americans. At Prego we were running with Eurotrash—we were cool."

Marsha ended up loving her time at MacArthur Park.

Larry's willingness to get into the muck and mire was evident in his personal life as well. When Michael was in high school in Ross, a town in Marin County, Larry saw more clearly than most parents where his son's crew's fledgling leisure pursuits had them headed. Although Larry didn't yet know many of the Ross guys' parents, he organized a weekday lunch at MacArthur Park—not for the dads, but for the moms. This was classic Larry: as much as he cherishes his male friendships, he readily allows that he may in fact prefer the company of women.

At the luncheon Larry tactfully shared what he knew of the boys' exploits. He educated and wowed the ladies, who returned to Marin a bit wiser, impressed by and appreciative of this hands-on father.

In a similar vein, daughter Laura once met Larry at the Front Street office, where he immediately steered her out the door for a "walk." In the most loving but direct way possible, he told her what he saw and knew about questionable behavior she was exhibiting and how it made him feel—more fearful and sad than angry. She already knew well his eagle eye from countless restaurant dinners where the light was too bright or the table wasn't set properly; now it was focused uncomfortably on her. Getting "found out" was upsetting, but further disappointing her father would have devastating.

By that time Spectrum had moved its headquarters from Pier 1 to upstairs from MacArthur Park at 617 Front Street, now home to the Koret Foundation. It was a very special block. A blindfolded cosmopolite would have likely known through her ears and nose alone that she was on Front between Jackson and Pacific. There was no traffic to speak of, and the distinctive, enticing aroma of ribs wafted out MacArthur Park's smoker.

In January 1984 Michael Dellar joined Spectrum Foods as vice president of marketing and business development. Michael came from Oakland household products giant Clorox, where he had directed marketing for the restaurant division, primarily for the eleven Emil Villa's Hick'ry Pit restaurants in the Bay Area and Seattle.

A big part of Michael's job was to help Larry and Franco dream up new concepts, scout possible locations, and negotiate deals. Business was booming in San Francisco for Spectrum, bolstered by the Major League Baseball All-Star Game and the Democratic National Convention in the summer of 1984, as well as the Super Bowl at Stanford in early 1985. Larry wanted to keep it rolling.

Spectrum opened a new spot in Los Angeles as it was preparing to host the 1984 Summer Olympics. About a year earlier, Larry and Debby were in Italy with Jerry and Lois, along with several of Spectrum's native-born Italian chefs and managers. The trips kept Chianti, Harry's, Ciao, and Prego current and authentically Italian. They were a joyful "grind" of endurance eating and drinking. *La dolce vita*. Someone had to do it.

The group's final dinner, at one of Florence's hottest new restaurants, figured to be the fortnight's high point. One of the Italians—perhaps it was Franco, maybe it was Luciano Bardinelli, no one remembers exactly—was in charge of the reservation. Italian was their first language, and they often knew someone who knew someone connected to the restaurant, which made things flow more smoothly.

When the group arrived, the host had no reservation in their name. There was no table for the Spectrum party.

His heart set on dinner there that night, one of the men went ballistic, barking at the host. Larry took a different angle, quietly conveying how eager everyone was to eat there and asking if there wasn't some way they could be accommodated.

The host thought for a moment and said, "We do have one other table, but no customer has ever sat there before. It's the employee meal table in the kitchen. You wouldn't want to sit there, would you?"

He took Larry into the kitchen and showed him the table. Larry agreed to the unorthodox setup, a decision he did not regret, neither in the short term—the meal was magnificent—nor in the long run.

As they made their way through the delicious dinner smack dab in the middle of the chaotic hustle and bustle of the kitchen, Larry realized the experience was far from second-rate. It was like snagging a backstage pass offering live sensory stimulation—sight, sound, and smell—that a quiet dining room, however nice, could not provide.

That experience led to Spectrum's newest Los Angeles restaurant. Chianti had long needed a bigger kitchen. Larry realized they could get that kitchen and a "new" restaurant at the same time—and in the same building—if they gave up the storeroom-turned-office that cost-conscious Chuck had so cleverly created a decade before—especially if they didn't have to build a wall between the expanded kitchen and the dining room.

The "new" restaurant was called Chianti Cucina (*cucina* means "kitchen" in Italian). It was intended to serve the same clientele as Chianti, but in a less formal, more simple and relaxed setting under the same roof.

The tiled, trattoria-like space had an open kitchen and would only seat forty. The same kitchen served both Chianti and Cucina, and patrons could order from either menu.

Whether Larry knew it or not, he was once again ahead of the curve, anticipating society's turn towards less formality. He was meeting people where they were, while never compromising on food, service, or value.

Cucina was an excellent example of Larry "being open" to something, a phrase used regularly in his conversations; or, more specifically, "if you're open to it." Life often presents situations that at first glance might appear neutral or even negative. For those like Larry who can roll with them, they can contain valuable lessons, if not end up being blessings in disguise.

Larry could have turned on his heel and stomped off that night in Florence when the restaurant had no table for his party. Instead, he hung with it, calmly made his case to the host, accepted a table that many diners—particularly prominent restaurateurs—would have refused, and enjoyed a fabulous one-night experience, one that turned into a lasting and very profitable business idea—all because he was *open to it*.

In so doing he helped show the world that informal wasn't necessarily inferior; it, too, could be stimulating and tasteful.

Chuck Frank opened Cucina with Umberto Gibbin. Umberto, like *maestro* Franco Galli, was a veteran "cruise ship Italian." He was briefly assistant manager at Ciao, before moving to Los Angeles to become Chianti's general manager.

"Larry was in Italy, and he told Umberto and me to create a lunch menu, but to use the Chianti menu for dinner," he explained. "Lunch was fine the first day, but no one was interested when we handed them the Chianti dinner menu at night. Umberto and I decided we should run the same menu all day, even though Larry had suggested otherwise. We went from no one the first day, to one couple the second, to 240 covers in a forty-seat space the third day. It was crazy, a huge success."

One day in 1984 a car pulled up to Chianti as the lunch rush subsided. Two men walked in, wearing a combination of *il Tricolore*—the green, white, and red of the Italian flag. The men were the president and the secretary of the Italian Water Polo Federation, in Los Angeles for the Olympics. They wondered whether the restaurant could host the entire team for a meal. Umberto replied Cucina would be delighted to have them. He was filled with pride when the hunky, well-fueled team went on to win a silver medal.

Umberto was also working at Chianti one night the year before, when a handsome movie star—a regular—came in for dinner. Visit after visit, he sat in the same booth, enchanting what seemed to be a different companion every time. The actor once asked Debby's sister Eleanor out. She replied, "Sure, sounds great. Want to meet my parents?"

This particular evening, the actor's waiter was puzzled: the couple was no longer at the table. He asked Umberto if the star had left without saying goodbye—or paying—which would have been very unlike the typically generous and gregarious man. Umberto insisted they could not have left—they would have had to walk past him at the podium.

The waiter took another look. He saw two pair of shoes neatly lined up and heard soft but telling noises coming from under the table, even as the fine white tablecloth obscured his view of the duo's calisthenics.

With Cucina up and roaring, Larry began to open himself and Spectrum to something far bigger than in-kitchen dining. An investment banking firm approached him, wondering if he had ever considered taking his company public. Larry had thought about it from time to time, but he wasn't interested. He didn't believe that Spectrum was ready—physically or psychologically—for growth of that magnitude; it lacked the infrastructure to support a public offering. Larry preferred the seat-of-the-pants autonomy and flexibility that came with remaining private.

Several weeks later the bankers returned.

"How would you feel," they asked, "about being acquired by a billion-dollar New York Stock Exchange industry leader?"

They worked with Menlo Park-based Saga Corporation. Saga's bread and butter—pun intended—was institutional food service: hospitals, schools, and hotels. But they also had a $350-million-dollar restaurant division.

Saga wanted to buy Spectrum primarily for the "culture" at the group's restaurants, but also because they wanted Larry. He would come aboard as new president of Saga's restaurant division, which would include Spectrum, as well as Velvet Turtle, a semi-formal fine-dining establishment famous for its cold cucumber soup, beef Wellington, and iconic bespectacled-tortoise-in-top-hat-and-bow-tie logo; Stuart Anderson's Black Angus Western-themed steak restaurants; the Straw Hat Pizza chain; and others.

The bankers floated one additional inducement: Saga's legendary CEO, Charlie Lynch, had long admired Larry and believed him to be a viable heir apparent. There was a good chance that within the next few years Larry would be running the entire corporation.

Larry was flattered and intrigued. As chairman of Spectrum he also had a fiduciary responsibility to consider the offer from a broader perspective: would it be good for Jerry and the other investors? The employees? Other potential buyers had approached Spectrum before, but they had been easy to brush aside. He didn't want to sell. He liked having control. Spectrum was his baby. Saga—and Lynch in particular—however, were difficult suitors to dismiss. Selling might be good not only for Larry, but also for the Spectrum family.

Larry agreed to meet Charlie, privately and confidentially. The meeting went well and led to another—just the two men—where Charlie proposed that Saga buy Spectrum for $14 million. Larry would become president of Saga's restaurant division. He would still oversee "his" restaurants, but he also would be on track to perhaps someday take the helm at Saga. It felt right.

He looked Charlie in the eye, shook his hand, and said, "Thank you very much. I will bring your offer to Jerry and the board."

For their money, in addition to Spectrum's special "culture" and Larry himself, Saga would get nine restaurants employing 600 men and women. Listed in chronological order by opening date, they included: Chianti, MacArthur Park, Harry's Bar, Ciao, MacArthur Park Palo Alto, Prego, Prego Beverly Hills, MacArthur Park Huntington Beach, and Chianti Cucina.

Spectrum was unique. Larry objected when people would call it a chain. He believed that sold short Spectrum's chefs and general managers. Even though the MacArthur Parks and the Pregos shared the same names and menus, respectively, each interior was separately designed from the ground up. Each was run by an empowered, entrepreneurially oriented management team. Spectrum offered these men and women significant creative freedom, as well as profit sharing. They did not have to fit into some predetermined corporate mold.

San Francisco Chronicle food critic—and accomplished restaurateur in her own right—Patricia Unterman said that Spectrum launched "high-quality, managerially enlightened restaurants, the most innovative segment of the chain-restaurant business."

And of course, Chianti, Harry's Bar, Ciao, and Cucina were all unique, stand-alone restaurants.

Larry preferred the word "group" to "chain," eventually accepting that by most of the world's shorthand, Spectrum was a chain, whatever—to his mind inaccurate—slight denigration that implied. Sometimes he even quoted noted food and wine critic Colman Andrews, who said Spectrum was "the thinking man's restaurant chain." Spectrum restaurants were independent, chef-partnered, one-offs. Each was built upon the same personal, fanatic commitment to quality that success in that industry demands—and each was different.

The chain designation did not account for the variety of Spectrum's offerings either. Ciao was radically different than MacArthur Park, even though they were but a twenty-second walk from each other. As Larry said in a 1984 letter to employees, "Some have suggested that we have written a new chapter in the fine-food industry by first conceiving and then managing not only multiple restaurants but also multiple food concepts. Perhaps history will show that we were the first to do so successfully—success being measured both by financial performance and by aesthetic excellence."

While Larry and Charlie Lynch were discussing Saga's desire to buy Spectrum, Jerry had a heart attack. Larry flew to Los Angeles and visited him in the hospital, where he was on his way to a full recovery. Larry himself still had mixed feelings about the possible sale—it was hard to imagine someone else having ultimate say over his baby—but Jerry's response to the proposed offer settled those feelings and clarified his thinking. Jerry asked Larry to agree to the sale. That request, made by a dear friend from his hospital bed following a near-death experience, made Larry's choice all the easier.

Larry accepted the offer. It was an exciting time for the man whose company in its early days had flirted with insolvency far more often than he wished. All that was left was for the bankers and lawyers to cross the *t*'s and dot the *i*'s.

Several days later Larry answered his car phone—still primarily an executive tool in 1984, since the jabbering masses had not yet joined the collective conversation—and heard an unfamiliar voice.

It was an associate of Charlie's, a man Larry had never met. He said that he had examined Spectrum's books more closely than Charlie. Because of the new MacArthur Park Huntington Beach's sluggish start, Saga would now pay $12 million for Spectrum, not the $14 million Larry and Charlie had agreed upon.

Larry couldn't believe it. Who was this guy? He'd never even heard of him. Larry and Charlie had a deal, sealed with a handshake and a look in the eye. For Midwesterner Larry, a man's word was his bond, superseding all else.

Setting aside his shock and fury, Larry told the caller he had agreed to $14 million with Charlie. If that was no longer the deal, Spectrum was not for sale.

The man tried to explain why Saga had changed its terms. Larry heard him out but stood firm.

"Charlie and I had a deal. We shook hands. That's as good as a notarized signature to me. If he wants to go back on that, I'm sorry, no sale."

In a surprised and almost sympathetic tone that conveyed *good luck with that, no chance*, the man agreed to relay the message.

Larry bashed his steering wheel in frustration, yanking loose the horn assembly.

"I felt the heat from my brain to my feet. I was so mad—more at myself than at Charlie. All I could think was, *You just turned down $12 million. Are you out of your effing mind?* But then I calmed down. I knew I had done it out of principle rather than ego or greed. If that lost us the deal, so be it. We were still a good company. I believed in right and wrong, and I believed in Spectrum. We had such good people."

A few hours later the man called back.

"I talked to Charlie. He agrees with you. A deal is a deal. The sale price is $14 million."

A wave of relief and exhilaration washed over Larry.

He thought back to his father's initial skepticism when Larry told him he and Jerry were buying Chianti. He remembered the daunting days at Chianti before Lois Dwan's crucial review; The Green House and investor hassles; bag lady Barbara Frank having to mule money from one bank to another. He recalled the night he took Michael, Laura, and Tony—ages ten, eight, and five—to Giovanni's Pizza in Sausalito and told them Spectrum would likely go bankrupt.

Laura asked, "What's that word mean?"

Mike explained, "That we're going to lose all our money."

From a contemporary parenting perspective, arguably a tad more information than the tykes needed. But, as Larry later reflected, "Those kids were my everything."

He thought, too, of Debby's comforting reaction to the news: "That's okay, honey. We'll move to a cheaper house, and I'll go back to teaching."

All of those ulcer-inducing close calls were part of a stressful but rewarding history with an eminently satisfying ending. Spectrum and Larry had overcome myriad obstacles and won. He was ecstatic, if still a little disbelieving, a bewilderment that quickly vanished when the wire cleared .

Following the sale, life didn't change much for most Spectrum employees. The restaurants operated as usual, and, as Larry wrote, "Spectrum's management team won't change, Chuck will still be signing your paycheck, the *maestro* (Franco) will still be orchestrating his wonderful food; Mark Walker, director of American operations, will still be managing with the managers; Michael Dellar will still be searching for new sites and marketing existing restaurants; and, to the extent his health permits, Jerry will still be advising, guiding, and being a trusted friend to many of us—especially me. Finally, our corporate office will remain at 617 Front Street, and my door is still open for anyone who wants to drop by. I am glad each of you will be here to help make the next chapter as successful as the others in our family history."

Larry was the exception to the general continuity. His day-to-day routine changed greatly. He still oversaw Spectrum, but he also had new and plentiful responsibilities at Saga in Menlo Park. In the twenty-two short months he worked there, Larry racked up five speeding tickets on a deserted, pre-tech-boom Interstate 280.

Almost everyone doubted that independent Larry would enjoy working for Saga—or any company not his own. He himself was excited and up for the challenge. He liked, respected, and saw an opportunity to learn from Charlie.

Saga had recently been named one of the "100 Best Companies to Work for in America." Larry's new office was huge with a great view. And he had never forgotten former UCLA chancellor and *Times Mirror* chairman Franklin Murphy's advice. He counseled YPO members to consider "repotting" themselves every seven years, like a gardener repots a growing plant. Western Coffee Instants and Caswell were shorter stints than his Spectrum run, but Larry had grown from previous occupational uprootings. He was open to all that his new employer might offer.

Larry ended up loving Saga, and Charlie in particular, whom he called, "The only boss I ever had."

Long after the men fell out of touch, ninety-seven-year-old Charlie, still playing nine holes every day, ate at one of Larry's restaurants. He left a warm note for his former protégé.

Larry's time at Saga was brief but pivotal. He would always recall fondly Spectrum's chaos, but he felt his executive capacity and confidence grow in Saga's "more thoughtful and responsible" environment. He met smart and accomplished people, and he learned a tremendous amount about the challenges and benefits of running a public rather than private company.

Larry worked harder than ever, giving Saga his all. But his time there was also something of a breather. Reporting to Charlie wasn't the restrictive or emasculating burden some had predicted it would be for lifelong boss Larry; often it was actually a relief. The buck no longer stopped completely with him. Someone else he respected and trusted shared and sometimes owned responsibilities Larry was used to shouldering by himself.

Although Larry remained the classic plucky underdog (in his own words, "just a little Jewish boy from Toledo"), the sale to Saga brought a measure of financial security. Daily work was no longer intricately tied to his longtime fear of going *mechula*, or bankrupt, as it had been for so long, the wolf always at the door. The security was a pleasant and salutary new reality.

One grandchild struggled to reconcile Larry's go-to underdog characterization with the confident, successful man he'd always known. Having heard enough to know that Larry's childhood was more comfortable than it was hardscrabble, he asked, "But didn't Eula Mae (Larry's mother's helper) make your bed every day?"

Although Larry's family's circumstances were indeed comfortable, in comparison some of his friends' families were *very* well-off. One father was a top executive at automotive glass manufacturer Libby-Owens-Ford, another owned the Chevy dealership.

"I wanted to be rich," he later recollected, clarifying that he long felt himself more a geographic and cultural long shot than an economic one.

"In my mind, I basically started out as a nobody from nowhere."

That same grandchild who asked about Eula Mae, having heard "little Jewish boy from Toledo" over and over again, turned it into Larry's own contemporary acronym, LJBFT.

As a division of Saga with access to the larger company's deeper pockets, Spectrum Foods was in a better position to grow. They could—and shareholders expected them to—open more restaurants more quickly than ever before. The trick would be to maintain Spectrum's signature quality and originality.

Larry was spending lots of time trying to turn around Saga's faltering Stuart Anderson's Black Angus Steakhouse and Velvet Turtle chains—getting back to basics, including dumping the add-on discotheques a prior consultant had championed. But he was also still engaged with his trusted Spectrum gang as they worked to expand.

This engagement included a research trip to Mexico, similar to the Italy trips. The brain trust—Larry, Jerry, architect Ron Nunn, Franco, and Michael Dellar—were developing Spectrum's latest restaurant, Guaymus, named after a village on the Sea of Cortez. By then fisherman and boater Larry had almost as strong an emotional tie to coastal Mexico as he did to Italy.

According to Michael Dellar, late one night the group was enjoying postprandial coffee and dessert after one of their south-of-the-border tasting dinners, when Larry's enthusiasm struck.

"This coffee is amazing. We *have* to serve it at Guaymus. I told you: these trips pay for themselves, they help separate us from the pack. We come down here and experience things firsthand."

He raised his cup—which may have been fortified by a splash of Kahlua—and toasted, "*A la vida! A la autenticidad!* (*To life! To authenticity!*)"

Franco went back into the kitchen and, using a combination of sign language, Italian, and English, got the Spanish-speaking staff to show him their secret, an incredible proprietary blend: a jar of Nescafe instant!

Guaymus opened in 1986 on the Belvedere-Tiburon downtown waterfront. Although Larry's son Michael hadn't yet officially kicked off his restaurant business career, he and his friends did their part to help get Guaymus going. He celebrated his twenty-first birthday there a week before it opened to the public, a dress rehearsal for staff.

Michael's friends boarded Larry's boat, the *Mindy*, at the St. Francis Yacht Club, not far from Mimi's house in the Marina, then cruised across the bay. His Aunt Gayle commandeered the boat's sound system, playing "We Are the World" on continuous repeat, before the group debarked at the Tiburon ferry dock, steps from the unfinished restaurant.

To acknowledge and even poke fun at the behind-schedule build-out, each guest was handed his own white plastic replica of a construction helmet, with "MICHAEL'S 21st" emblazoned in green across the crown.

Other guests drove rather than boated. The designated-driver concept was in its infancy; ride-sharing was decades away. One early-departing couple got pulled over by the Tiburon police. The officer likely weighed several factors as he waited for dispatch to run the driver's license, including the fresh-faced couple's evident terror and respect for the law, as well as their actual degree of threat to community safety. Making a small-town judgement call he could never make today, the patrolman directed the pair to leave the car where it was and walk the short distance back to the party. They were to remain there however long it took to clear their heads.

Guaymus was an immediate smash, hand over fist, but mostly on the weekends. As a result, staffing presented a real challenge for the general manager, Marsha. Guaymus needed twenty waiters on Friday, Saturday, and Sunday, but only five the rest of the week. That made it difficult to keep everyone happy. Marsha nonetheless found a way, just as she found a way to keep the waterfront building's temperamental plumbing operable—often by plunging the toilets herself.

She also found a way to keep Guaymus's gorgeous but not-so-bright star bartender on staff. He was popular with customers—women flocked to the restaurant because of him. She routinely stayed until 2:00 a.m. helping him close out his register, an hour after the other servers and bartenders had departed.

While Marsha was plunging toilets, Larry was being honored by the Italian government with the Caterina de Medici Medal, a significant distinction. He was the first American and the first person of non-Italian descent to receive the honor, which recognizes excellence in the preservation of Italian heritage outside of Italy. This was on the strength of Chianti, Harry's Bar, Ciao, and Prego; Il Fornaio, Poggio, and Convivo were yet to come.

Florence-born Caterina was the great-granddaughter of Lorenzo the Magnificent (fittingly enough, "Lorenzo" is "Larry" in Italian). Her arranged marriage made her the wife of sixteenth century French king Henry II, as well as the mother of three French kings: Francis II, Charles IX, and Henry III. She did much to promote Italian culture—gastronomy in particular—when she lived abroad in France. That the Italian government considered Larry her spiritual descendant spoke volumes. Little did he know it would also lead to a dinner with the captivating actress Sophia Loren.

Spectrum Takeout

Spectrum was exceptionally collaborative, but if there were ever a time when Larry wasn't around and someone else had to make a call, Executive Vice President Chuck Frank—number two on the org chart—was that person. He moved up from Los Angeles and began to work out of the Front Street office when Larry went to Saga.

Chuck might not have been bartering meals for paint or carpet anymore, never mind figuring out what to do when the weekend's proceeds disappeared along with the two-thousand-pound safe. But he was still putting out fires, if on a slightly larger scale.

Chuck walked into work one day and learned that Spectrum was being sued by the gargantuan Campbell Soup Company. Campbell had introduced its Prego spaghetti sauce in 1981, the same year Spectrum's Prego San Francisco opened. Campbell insisted that they "were there first." With Prego sauce sales of $100 million in its first year, "might" looked to make "right" in this situation.

Campbell asserted that because they had recently bought Café Prego on Catalina Island, they had trademark rights to the name for restaurants as well as sauces.

Chuck and Spectrum's lawyers did some digging. They learned that Campbell had used a straw man to purchase the restaurant, a front guy who misrepresented himself as an independent operator with no connection to the soup giant.

The judge considered each side's argument. Understanding that the companies were in two different businesses—Campbell in soups and sauces, Spectrum in restaurants—he ruled in Spectrum's favor, although he did grant exclusive "Prego" rights to Campbell on the island of Catalina. Spectrum could build and operate Prego restaurants everywhere else.

Catalina had been the site of a memorable father-son outing several years before. For his twelfth birthday, Michael requested an adventure alone with Larry—no Laura or Tony, just the firstborn and his dad. They set out from Marina del Rey on Larry's Grand Banks and, several choppy hours later, neared the special island. Apparently, Larry's boat lacked a compass; or, if it had one, it did not function properly. The bold entrepreneur was unfazed.

"I knew *about* where Catalina was," he later laughed. "That was good enough."

Former San Francisco 49er linebacker and current front-office executive Keena Turner was a MacArthur Park regular, as were Condor Club legend Carol Doda and her "twin 44s."

Although Larry chugged right past Avalon, their intended destination, with its arcades and ice cream parlors that would have entertained Michael for hours, he eventually made safe harbor at the more primitive Isthmus of Catalina. He was more relieved than Michael knew. He had almost completely overshot the entire seventy-six-square-mile island, and he feared that he'd blown his son's trip when he missed Avalon. To the contrary, Michael was delighted.

"Dad, I saw a *buffalo*! And I got to use the radio! *This is Yankee Whiskey Foxtrot…*"

By late 1984 Chianti wasn't the only location in need of an update; it was workhorse MacArthur Park's turn. Two crews worked consecutive ten-hour shifts, 6:00 a.m. to 4:00 p.m. and 4:00 p.m. to 2:00 a.m., seven days a week, to transform the San Francisco flagship. Larry and Chuck became master mollifiers, giving patient ear to neighbors who would call or even, in some cases, come to the office to gripe about the noise and the hours. "I understand," each would say, "I wouldn't like it either. We're so close, though, please bear with us."

They didn't tell the neighbors—let alone any work-stopping historians or anthropologists—about the remnants of a ship the crews discovered when excavating storage space beneath the restaurant. Instead, they decided to cart out the ship piece by piece.

607 Front Street, like much of the Barbary Coast neighborhood, was built on bay fill. Hundreds of ships that had transported miners and supplies during the Gold Rush never made the return trip to their ports of origin. Sunk at anchor along the waterfront, they eventually ended up buried beneath the fill that created several blocks of new buildable land.

When the restaurant construction crew completed its work—down to the wire, but on schedule—Larry took the blueprints and permit to city hall, as confident as an honor roll student about to receive his diploma that he would get the fire department's sign-off.

In an unexpected gut punch, the fire department functionary wouldn't sign off. Important elements like the Ansul R-102 Liquid Agent Fire Suppression System were in place, but the administrator got hung up on a minor misinterpretation of another issue.

Fuming as he strode up Van Ness to his car, Larry ran into Willie Brown, at that time Speaker of the California State Assembly. Brown later dated Kamala Harris and served as San Francisco mayor.

Power broker Brown was a Spectrum regular.

"Hey, Larry, what's shaking?"

"Willie, I've got the weight of the world and sixty of your constituents—our employees—on my shoulders. The fire department just kicked me in the nuts. They won't let us reopen, even though we are ready to go, safely. We're supposed to reopen tonight. I don't know what the problem is—some ridiculous red tape—but I have got to get my people back to work. They need to buy groceries and pay rent."

Brown turned to his aide.

"Write this down. I'm in the mood for ribs. Tonight. 7:00 p.m., four people. I want my ribs! You get that? And you hear me, Larry? 7:00 p.m. tonight. Don't forget—I'll see you there."

Ninety minutes later, a fire marshal dropped by the restaurant with the signed permit. Speaker Brown and his friends enjoyed their ribs that evening; a meal Willie never forgot, nor did he let Larry forget. From that night on the restaurateur became a supporter in checkbook if not always political mind or heart.

Saga Sale

Around this time Michael Dellar was very busy. He had on his plate new concept and product development, as well as the associated construction, design, lease negotiation, and subsequent marketing new endeavors entailed.

Spectrum expanded to the East Bay, opening Spiedini in Walnut Creek in 1986, as well as a San Francisco Harry's Bar and American Grill at McAllister and Van Ness, across from city hall, the Opera House, and Davies Symphony Hall. Spectrum also opened Spuntino, a casual bakery and pizzeria next door to Harry's, at the mouth of Redwood Alley, which was home to Jeremiah Tower's renowned Stars; and Tutto Bene as well, farther north on Van Ness."

One day in early May 1986, Larry and Charlie Lynch were on stage in an auditorium near Chicago, participating in a question-and-answer session with several hundred Saga employees. The men traveled throughout the country periodically, fielding questions from rank-and-file workers. This was exciting, a big deal to Larry. Part way through the session, when another division head was at the podium, a staffer brought Charlie a note. He read it, then nudged Larry and whispered, "Saga is in play."

"Oh," said Larry, not wanting to divert the audience's attention from the speaker. Possibilities raced through his head.

When there was a break, Larry asked Charlie, "Is that good or bad?"

"Bad. Very bad."

"I didn't know then. I was so naïve," Larry later laughed.

By "in play" Charlie meant that another company wanted to buy Saga. From his point of view that was bad, because it implied the other company had decided it could do a better, more profitable job of running Saga than Charlie. It was a performance review of sorts. He would most likely be out of a job if someone else bought the company.

On May 7 Saga announced that Marriott Corporation—a $3 billion hotel chain that, like Saga, also had a contract food service division, led by airport mainstay Host International—made an offer to purchase all of Saga's stock for $435 million in cash. The offer was for $34 a share, $4.50 higher than Saga's $29.50-a-share closing price on the New York Stock Exchange that day.

Marriott wanted Saga for its food service division, which accounted for most of its revenue and profits. In the United States and Canada no one fed more college students, corporate employees, and health-care-institution patients and workers than Saga.

In the lead-up to the sale, Marriott's chairman, Bill Marriott, and executive vice president, Butch Cash, met with each Saga division president. They were still trying to figure out whether they wanted to hold onto Saga's restaurant division if the acquisition went through. It was a side dish in their mind, compared to the main meal, the volume-feeding division.

Cash asked Spectrum president Chuck Frank what Marriott could do to help.

"Nothing. Just leave us alone, and we'll continue to thrive," Chuck replied.

Cash then asked what type of demographic studies Spectrum used to select locations, believing that the established giant could help with that. Chuck, channeling the Mimi-inspired early MacArthur Park, said, "Actually, Butch, here's our research: we walk into a location, touch the floor, feel the walls, and if the building talks to us, we move forward."

Cash rolled his eyes and whispered something to his associate. Chuck reported this back to Larry, who smiled.

When Marriott and Cash met with Larry, they asked how he would feel about continuing to run not just the Saga restaurants but all Marriott's existing restaurants as well. They acted as if it would be the simplest, most desirable thing in the world for Larry, new mom Debby (Nick was born June 5, 1986), and four-year-old Katherine to move to Washington, DC, where Marriott was headquartered.

That was an easy decline for Larry. He was rooted in San Francisco and Marin, with no desire to become a corporate transplant, following supposed opportunities—to work for others—across the country. Larry had always determined his own fate; being at the mercy of developments he could not influence did not appeal. Part of the draw to Saga had been the possibility he would assume Charlie's role. That was out the window.

What he wanted, from the moment he learned Saga was for sale, was to buy back Spectrum. He knew that Marriott wanted Saga for its institutional food service division and that it might be willing—might *want*—to sell the restaurants it was getting as part of the deal. Jerry had fully recovered from his heart attack and favored a Spectrum redux as well.

As the days went by, it became clear that Marriott intended to sell the restaurant division if and when they bought Saga, due at least in some part to their inability to entice Larry to join them in Washington, DC.

Larry and Jerry hired San Francisco investment banker Warren Hellman to represent them in negotiations with Marriott. Warren was as down-to-earth as he was smart and accomplished. His estate underwrites the free-in-perpetuity Hardly Strictly Bluegrass festival in Golden Gate Park.

Talks proceeded, and Larry and Jerry's excitement mounted, as did that of their friends at Spectrum. It would be the best of both worlds: dozens of people would reap the financial benefits of not one but two buyouts, the second completely unexpected—Spectrum to Saga, then Saga to Marriott—in two short years. They would also regain the freedom and autonomy they had previously enjoyed when Spectrum was a private company, minus some of the often-harrowing financial ups and downs that came along with it.

Larry was very pleased when Marriott and Cash agreed to the verbal offer for Spectrum that he, Jerry, and Hellman put together. However, he was furious days later when Marriott announced—on the same day it bought Saga for $502 million—that it planned to sell Spectrum, Stuart Anderson's Black Angus, Velvet Turtle, and Grandy's (described by one financial analyst as "an also-ran in the KFC business") to a group led by Anwar Soliman for $260 million.

Bill Marriott's alleged chicanery doesn't greatly shock at this distance, even if one might expect more from a pillar of the Mormon church. The Spectrum sale likely would not have netted more than $30 million tops, and Marriott would still have the considerably bigger Stuart Anderson's and Grandy's to unload. Soliman offered to take them all off their hands for a very nice price. It's not difficult to see why Marriott and Cash cooled on Larry and Jerry's non-binding offer.

Jerry and Larry still going strong.

To Larry, however, this was another version of the Spectrum-to-Saga sale, when Charlie's subordinate said the actual sale price would be two million dollars less than the number sealed with a handshake. Fiddling with a deal—or outright reneging on it—did not compute for Larry; he was enraged, his fury only increasing when some speculated Marriott had been in quiet talks with Soliman while also negotiating with Larry, possibly using him for the sole purpose of establishing the market value for Spectrum. Adding insult to injury, a front-page headline in *Nation's Restaurant News* proclaimed, "Soliman Outbids Mindel for Saga Restaurants."

Anwar was known for his ambition. A 1987 *Los Angeles Times* headline read "Soliman's Appetite for Restaurants: Master Dealmaker Hopes to Build a Company that Will Rival McDonald's." Once he made the deal with Marriott, he headed north to Menlo Park to assess his purchase and meet with restaurant personnel at Saga headquarters. Charlie Lynch asked Larry to show Anwar around. Larry snapped, "Show him around yourself." He relented when Charlie asked him to do so as a personal favor.

As they toured the campus, Anwar—likely recognizing that Larry, who had long been the dynamic face of Spectrum and possessed a personal presence different than his own—worked hard to recruit Larry. He wanted Larry to join him in purchasing Spectrum, Stuart Anderson's Black Angus, Velvet Turtle, Grandy's, and Spoons from Marriott.

Larry had no interest. All he wanted was to get Spectrum back. Although Black Angus was Saga's bell cow, generating more than two thirds of the restaurant division's revenues (117 units), almost everyone believed that the considerably smaller but hipper, more sophisticated Spectrum was the trophy Anwar was hunting—a trophy that would have considerably more luster with Larry.

"I want one of two things," Larry told Anwar. "I want my company back. If that can't happen, I want to challenge my non-compete agreement. I want to compete against you."

When Larry agreed to sell Spectrum to Saga he had signed a four-year non-compete agreement. Until the agreement expired in 1988, he would not leave Saga and open his own place in the four counties where Spectrum did business: San Francisco, Santa Clara, Los Angeles, or San Diego. The agreement remained in effect when Marriott spun off the restaurants to Anwar.

"And number three?" asked Anwar.

"There is no number three. Spectrum Foods will never be your company. It will always be mine."

"That's the maddest I have ever been in my life," Larry later reflected. "I was so upset. At the restaurant business, at life. I felt I had been done wrong. We had a deal with Marriott to buy back Spectrum, the company we built, and they double-crossed us as far as I was concerned, not honoring the oral agreement we had reached. I was furious. I'm from Toledo, Ohio, and in Toledo we don't go back on our word."

People knew Larry was angry. He told an interviewer that he was "openly hostile" to Anwar's purchase and that all of the key people at Spectrum would "want to leave" if the sale went through, a heat-of-the-moment statement he soon walked back.

"I hope my departure won't have any effect," he clarified. "If there are mass defections then I won't have built the organization I think I've built."

"Isn't that just capitalism?" an interviewer asked. "Marriott never signed anything binding with you, and Anwar offered them what they considered a better deal."

Larry laughed and said, "Yeah, capitalism's great until you do it to me."

It is easy to appreciate the self-awareness and self-acceptance in this response. Larry saw and could chuckle at the contradiction, while remaining true to the fiery competitor inside.

Marriott owned Spectrum for the briefest of moments. They announced the deal to sell the Saga restaurants to Soliman's American Restaurant Group on August 12, 1986, the same day they completed their $502-million purchase of Saga. They bought Saga knowing they were going to get rid of the restaurants; they were just a pass-through middleman of sorts. As such, they did not burn as deeply into Larry's psyche as Anwar did.

Soliman became the new "Mr. Spectrum Foods." He was not only the owner, but also Larry's nemesis—if not outright enemy.

"You have to understand. I felt like he stole my company, the company we built. Rational or not, that's how I felt," Larry explained. "Spectrum was who I was. It was the way I could speak to the world, through my wonderful associates. Spectrum was my wife. The employees were my family."

On October 9, 1986, Larry wrote a letter of resignation to all Spectrum employees, that said in part:

Good fortune and good people have made us successful. As we poured our energy and hearts into Spectrum, it never occurred to me that I would not always be able to shape its destiny. In business as in life, though, fate takes strange turns, and this time fate has determined that Spectrum and I, having literally grown up together, should now part company.

These past sixteen years have been the most wonderful of my life. What has made them virtually perfect are the people I have worked alongside, many for well over a decade, a special few since the day we started…I have been lucky enough to have spent these years surrounded by a loving family and supported by Spectrum's co-founder and my best friend, Jerry Magnin. What makes me even more blessed, though, is that my family extends to every single person at Spectrum. I care about all of you very much and will miss you all greatly.

Larry was done, but scores of his beloved associates continued to work for Spectrum, including Chuck as president. Twenty-four managers and chefs had long-term payouts coming after Anwar bought the company, and Chuck wanted to make sure those people were taken care of. The day all were finally made whole Chuck flipped Anwar the keys and said goodbye.

Larry was not idle long. Headhunters representing companies seeking strong leadership called regularly. He considered some offers, even going so far as to fly to Minneapolis to investigate one opportunity. That, however, was a tough sell, the frigid Minnesota winters even less appealing than the sticky Washington, DC summers.

Shortly after he distributed his Spectrum resignation letter, Larry walked into a very special ambush. Hundreds of family, friends, and former industry associates threw him a surprise going-away party at MacArthur Park. As he told *Nation's Restaurant News* columnist Alan Liddle, "It was the most wonderful night—businesswise—that I've ever had." Liddle wrote, "Mindel owned up to being rather sentimental as the high points and humorous experiences of his restaurant career were touched on by a number of speakers. 'I laughed a lot, but I cried more,' said Mindel. Charles Frank, a longtime Mindel associate, remarked that his ex-boss was not the only one with impaired vision:

'there were a lot of teary eyes.'"

Earlier in the year, just before Marriott put Saga in play, Larry learned that a house several doors down in Sausalito was for sale. Although he loved 100 San Carlos, the house he bought in 1971 and had lived in since, he had also long admired Hazel Mount, a "historic landmark view estate" at 86 San Carlos. When he heard it might be for sale, he walked over and introduced himself to the owners. The couple showed him around their wood-and-stucco Tudor home, one of Sausalito's first formal estates. Its vintage oak doors and stone fireplaces were shipped from England in the 1870s by the sea captain who developed the lot.

Larry fell hard but kept a poker face, even as he discreetly gulped when they mentioned an asking price of $1.5 million.

As he walked back home, the words "stock options" resounded in his head. When Saga bought Spectrum in 1984, they paid Larry in both cash and stock, common practice when a key executive joins an acquiring company. What's long-term good for the new corporation is also good for the executive, the thinking goes. The executive will be motivated to work hard and to remain with the company for a helpful interval, rather than coasting on their newly fattened wallet or walking away at sale.

Between the cash he received—and then prudently invested—in the 1984 Spectrum sale to Saga and the equity he had in his 100 San Carlos house, Larry could have swung the Hazel Mount purchase. But the house still felt expensive, beyond his reach—until he remembered the Saga stock options. He hadn't given them much thought while working in Menlo Park. They were sort of funny money, something over there in a corner that didn't count toward his net worth. He focused instead on the work at hand, making Black Angus, Velvet Turtle, and Spectrum as profitable as he could.

Now, as he realized that Marriott really was going to buy Saga, he did some quick calculations. The stock would convert to over a million dollars cash from the sale. He already knew that he wanted to buy back

Spectrum—maybe most of the million-dollar windfall would go right back into that. But the details didn't matter as much as the general feeling, call it consumer confidence: *I might actually have a little more money than I think I do. 86 San Carlos might not be the wishful-thinking or reckless-impulse buy my conscience assumes it to be. What if that could be our family's new home?*

Value has always been important to Larry, down to the gas pump. When he realized a local gas station, Shoreline Arco, consistently charged at least a few cents less per gallon than anyone else, he became a longtime customer, happy to wait a few minutes longer in their lines.

Value is one of the four legs of his famous restaurant stool: great food, excellent service, comfortable and beautiful atmosphere, and reasonable price. Diners should leave feeling their money was well spent.

As for 86 San Carlos, he didn't feel it was overpriced. It wasn't a gouge—the buyer would definitely get value. But it still felt frighteningly—and exhilaratingly—expensive. He had to, or *got to*, face the facts: he had worked extremely hard and been incredibly fortunate. Life had sent some very talented and special associates and opportunities his way, and now he was reaping the rewards.

Although Larry has always been a conservative spender, he has also long enjoyed treating himself or loved ones to "affordable luxuries"—a special cashmere sports coat, a performance automobile, a boat, 86 San Carlos, a getaway in Montana—that come *after* Larry has reached a targeted goal or is the beneficiary of a wonderful windfall. He does not live beyond his means, and although the rewards are nice in and of themselves, the risk, effort, shared history, and fortunate outcomes behind the booty make Larry's prosperity meaningful.

Debby told Larry she was perfectly content in their current house, but if buying 86 was something he really wanted to do, she would support the move. They took the plunge, closing on 86 San Carlos on May 22, 1986, right in the midst of the Saga-Marriott chaos. Nick was born June 5.

Larry's five children, clockwise from left: Tony, Mike, Laura, Nick, Katherine; Sausalito, 1986

Early Il Fornaio

Warren Hellman had known Larry socially or by business reputation prior to working together to try to buy back Spectrum from Marriott. Warren was impressed and began to wonder if Larry might not be the answer to one of his business dilemmas.

From Peter Graumann's 2001 special in the *San Francisco Chronicle*, "Il Fornaio: Translating Success from Italy to America":

> In 1972 in Barlissina—a small village outside of Milan—a family of furniture and fixture makers, committed to the goal of preserving the disappearing craft of Italian artisanal baking, created the Il Fornaio Baking School. Carlo Veggetti, who was managing Arredamenti Veggetti, S.p.A., the store fixture manufacturing works his great-grandfather had founded, opened the school as part of a strategy to stimulate ongoing demand for his family's shop fixtures, as well as enabling them to jump into the wholesale food business. Veggetti developed his concept of the 'neighborhood baker' into what eventually became the largest bakery chain in Italy. The first outlet opened in 1975; ten years later there were thousands of Il Fornaio bakeries throughout Italy.
>
> He and his family gathered centuries-old bread and pastry recipes from every region in Italy. In the school, bakers learned the methods needed to prepare these traditional recipes; furthermore, the school provided the baker-students with the materials for opening their own bakeries under the Il Fornaio name. The franchiser (Veggetti) provides end-to-end services including site development, training and marketing. 'This is very high-quality product, not for supermarkets—as good as homemade,' asserts Carlo's wife Silene, the firm's managing

director.

Later in the piece, Graumann writes:

> Howard Lester, chairman of San Francisco-based housewares/kitchenwares retailer Williams Sonoma, discovered the Il Fornaio bakeries during a business trip to Florence and fell in love with the Old World bakeries. He tracked down Carlo Veggetti and negotiated an agreement for the rights to Il Fornaio in North America (trademark and certain recipes).
>
> Il Fornaio's American experience began in 1981 with the opening of a bakery on San Francisco's Union Street (at Steiner, just down from Prego). The authentic Italian *pugliese* and *pannini* were gastronomical hits, encouraging Williams Sonoma to build seven more small bakeries in California. All interior fixtures and furnishings came from the Veggetti works in Italy, as did the recipes. Bakers were sent to Milan for training.

Customers loved the bakeries, but they were not profitable. The economic model made no sense; it was way too labor intensive. As Williams Sonoma prepared to go public in 1983, they needed to make themselves as attractive to new investors as possible. They decided to sell the unprofitable Il Fornaio bakeries.

Howard Lester still loved the bakeries—even as they lost money—and he believed that someday they could become profitable. So he reached into his own pocket, also convincing friends and acquaintances, including Warren Hellman, to join him in buying the bakeries from Williams Sonoma.

As acclaimed and beautiful as the bakeries were with Veggetti fixtures, they continued to lose money under new ownership, torpedoed in part by a revolving door of non-food-oriented CEOs, among them one who would later head Reebok shoes.

Although Larry's and his attempt to buy back Spectrum from Marriott had failed, Warren soon realized the experience might have provided a solution for the flailing Il Fornaio America bakeries and cafes. As they had fought hard, side by side, to regain Spectrum, Warren had seen Larry in action, up close and personal.

Over lunch at MacArthur Park one day in October 1986, shortly after Larry had distributed the Spectrum farewell letter, Warren asked him what he thought of the Il Fornaio bakeries and cafes. Specifically, he wondered if he saw a way for them to turn a profit.

Larry thought that, as wonderful and romantic—and *Italian*—as the idea of a small stand-alone bakery was—where people would shop every day, rather than going to the supermarket once a week—the economic model simply would not work in the U.S. The bakeries were too small. They could not generate enough revenue to pay the caliber of people—managers in particular—whom Larry considered one of the real keys to his success in the restaurant business.

"But if you attach this $600,000- or $700,000-a-year bakery and café to a $3- or $4-million-a-year restaurant, *now* you can afford to hire the right people."

Warren—and Howard, who was there, too—listened closely to what Larry had to say. Then they suggested he take over as CEO.

Larry thought for a moment before stating the following terms: he would get at least 51 percent of the company, all debt would be paid off by the time he took over, and the company would need to have $400,000 in the bank.

Warren and Howard accepted. They wrote out the agreement on the back of a MacArthur Park cocktail napkin, and all three men shook hands.

Larry had a track record. He was superb with people and with authentic Italian food. Warren and Howard likely preferred to own less of a profitable company than more of an unprofitable one. They were therefore willing to share ownership with the one man in America most capable of turning their underperforming dog into the money-making and highly acclaimed outfit they believed it might one day be. What did they have to lose, really? As Howard told the *Chronicle*, "I hope we'll make money in addition to good bread. We're so excited to have Larry. I think he's an unusually talented guy."

Larry understood that the deal could not be finalized until he talked to Carlo Veggetti. Williams Sonoma, and later Warren and Howard's group, owned the US rights to Il Fornaio America, but Veggetti was still the franchiser and had some say in how the business would be run.

Larry flew to Milan to meet Carlo. As Graumann went on to describe in his *San Francisco Chronicle* piece:

> Mindel came to the Veggetti family headquarters outside Milan with a plan to reorganize the money-losing Il Fornaio bakery in California (incorporating the bakeries into full-service restaurants).
>
> I was presenting tough terms including the elimination of franchise fees and a million-dollar loan in exchange for Carlo getting some equity,' recalls the dapper Mindel. 'After several days of getting nowhere, including one full day of cooling my heels in an unheated conference room waiting for Carlo to show up, I threatened to walk. Carlo asked what did I really want? I replied that I needed him to agree to my terms. He smiled, lifted his pen and wrote out his signature. He'd been testing me. I left the room liking him.'

When he returned to California, a newly reinvigorated Larry got to work putting together his team. He only needed a small crew at first, just a few people whose work he knew and trusted. If most of them were currently employed at Anwar's Spectrum, so much the sweeter. Larry felt gratified and vindicated when people like Franco Galli, Claudio Marchesan, Stanley Morris, and Valerie Stannard left solid situations at Spectrum to reunite with their old boss, mentor, comrade, and friend at what was basically an unguaranteed start-up.

The week before Thanksgiving, Larry went into Prego, which Stanley was managing at the time, and told him in confidence about his trip to meet with Veggetti in Milan, finishing with an inquiry that Stanley later said "would change the course of my life." Larry asked Stanley to join him at the new Il Fornaio (America) Corporation with—for the time being—just three other Spectrum people: *maestro* Franco, executive chef Claudio, and Larry's longtime assistant Valerie.

"I accepted. Without hesitation. Right on the spot."

Larry explained to Stanley that completing the deal and taking over the existing California Il Fornaio bakeries could take six or seven months. Excited to have a promising new job waiting for him a half-year down the line, Stanley gave notice the following week and made plans to take an extended sabbatical in Florence, where he would study Italian at the University of Florence, as well as food and culture. He would also study baking at Il Fornaio's headquarters outside of Milan. He left for Florence New Year's Day 1987.

Larry summoned him back to San Francisco in May. By June Stanley was working out of Il Fornaio's new North Beach office. Larry moved the company from an uninspiring, nondescript location in San Mateo to the heart of San Francisco's Italian neighborhood shortly after he took over.

"We had to change the culture," he explained. "We had to make it Italian."

Romano Chietti, the wine merchant who became part of Larry and Franco's "kitchen cabinet" at Ciao, introduced Larry to vendors Walter Guerra and Carlo Di Ruocco. Like Romano, Guerra and Di Ruocco were native Italians who in 1978 started food service businesses in the Bay Area. Their companies are thriving today. Chietti still shows up for work every morning at Siena Imports, now run by his son, Jason. Guerra's Ital Foods became the largest importer of Italian foods on the West Coast. Di Ruocco's pioneering Mr. Espresso, specializing in espresso machine imports and service, continues to be a key player in its niche.

Romano also introduced Larry to Gino Biradelli, one of several unofficial "mayors of North Beach" and owner of the Cafferata Ravioli Factory on Columbus Avenue. Romano, Gino, Walter, and Carlo, along with Franco, Claudio, Umberto, and other Italians at Spectrum, enhanced Larry's growing *paisan* credibility. Larry wasn't a cook. He didn't come up through the kitchen as so many "real" Italian restaurant owners did. He wasn't from Italy or San Francisco originally. In a culture that revolved around "knowing a guy," it was helpful to have insider friends and business associates who respected and vouched for him, who recognized in this Midwesterner a real Italian at heart, a true brother.

Gino set Larry up with the office on Filbert Street, just down from Washington Square and Saints Peter and Paul Church, directly across from Joe DiMaggio Playground Park. He also began to invite Larry to his famous "Italians only" Saturday lunches in the cellar of his hundred-year-old Caferrata Ravioli Factory, where Romano, Walter, and Carlo were regulars. It was yet another step on the road to figurative "made man."

Larry, Franco, Valerie, Stanley, and Claudio worked hard in the new office, preparing to open the first Il Fornaio restaurant. They were soon joined by another "defector," Spectrum's brand and graphics manager, Hilary Wolf, as well as wine buff and foodie Ed Levine, a recent Stanford MBA who would serve as vice president of finance.

When Larry and Jerry bought Chianti, there was no long-range plan to create what ultimately became the sixteen-restaurant Spectrum Foods. At first, they just hoped to make a go of Chianti—initially a very open question.

Il Fornaio was different. Larry now had a superb track record and a national reputation, and he had Warren and Howard, as well as institutional investors Wells Fargo Bank and InterWest, a venture capital firm. The plan was to create a replicable concept and, with direct access to expansion funding, to grow.

That summer of 1987, *The San Francisco Chronicle* wrote, "If all goes well—and with Hellman's backing—Mindel expects Il Fornaio to be a $50 million company (more than 10 times its current size) in five years."

Il Fornaio was serious business for Larry. But, as always with him, there were emotional components at play, too. The competitor in him rejoiced every time another associate left Spectrum to join Il Fornaio—*take that, Anwar!* In more of a Norman Rockwell vein, Larry loved taking over a bakery chain. It brought back memories of World War II, going to the Jewish part of Toledo on Sunday mornings with his father, Sy, to buy just-baked bagels.

"The bagels themselves were a treat," Larry reminisced. "Anything like that during the war was a treat. But maybe more than anything, I just loved being with my dad."

Larry likely was alluding to those outings when he told the *Examiner*, "No matter how large the business grows, the company will continue to bake its goods the old-fashioned way. It's an emotional business. It's hard work. It's tedious. It's very inefficient. But that's why the bread tastes so good."

The four-year non-compete agreement Larry signed when he

sold Spectrum to Saga in 1984 was still in effect when Larry joined Il Fornaio.

"I became an asset. I feel a little bit like a baseball player under contract," he joked to the *Chronicle*.

Under the terms of the agreement, he could not open a restaurant in San Francisco, Santa Clara, Los Angeles, or San Diego counties until late 1988. In 1984 he had signed the agreement as a matter of transactional course, never thinking he would want to open his own place so soon after. Far from it, at the time he imagined himself in 1987 happily working with Charlie Lynch at Saga, if not as Saga's CEO.

Looking at sites outside the excluded four counties, Larry felt shackled—exactly the point of the non-compete. He had his doubts about every location he visited, none more so than a shopping center in Corte Madera, a few exits up Highway 101 from his Sausalito home.

It *was* nearby—appealing to the involved father of a five-year-old daughter and a one-year-old son—and affluent Marin County residents had the means to dine out regularly. *But a shopping mall?* he asked himself, a space adjacent to JCPenny and Woolworth's? He was used to Spectrum's tonier locations.

Still, he did not want to sit around passively waiting for the non-compete to expire—that wasn't his way. With further growth on the horizon, he wanted and needed to prove the concept now. He would be free to work more fertile ground soon enough. The important thing was to get started, to show the dining public what Il Fornaio could be. He decided to roll the dice on Corte Madera, taking over a site previously occupied by a failed French restaurant.

Although Larry spared little expense when it came to the interior—"stunning marble and terra cotta floors and counters, delicately hand-painted walls, vaulted ceilings, and rich, dark wood," wrote the *San Francisco Chronicle's* Patricia Unterman—he told those who questioned the expenditures that the look was timeless and would endure, providing value in the end. His goal was to create a "sophisticated yet informal and friendly atmosphere intended to be suitable for a variety of meal occasions." Thirty-five years later it's safe to say he nailed it.

Another *Chronicle* columnist, Ruthe Stein, cited "the Mindel Touch," which she said meant "attention to every detail, from the marinade on the *bistecca alla fiorentina* to the shine on the Carrara-marble tile floors." A third publication said that Larry was "alert to the tonic effect of stylish surroundings."

In Larry's vision, guests in Corte Madera would be treated to olfactory as well as visual delights. They would see the open kitchen as they entered: rabbit, chicken, and leg of lamb slowly turning on the rotisserie (*giraorrosto*) over an open fire; steaks, chops, and fish cooking on the grill underneath; chefs tossing pizza crusts into the air before sliding them on wooden paddles into the wood-burning oven. And, whether they were consciously aware of it or not, diners would also smell the delectable aromas permeating throughout.

Of course, Larry didn't draw up the actual plans; architect Howard Backen did that. Backen was quite accomplished, with Robert Redford's Sundance Institute in Utah, George Lucas's Skywalker Ranch in Nicasio, and Delancey Street Foundation's headquarters on San Francisco's Embarcadero already to his credit. Larry and Howard had hit it off several years earlier, which led to Howard designing Larry and Debby's 86 San Carlos remodel. That, in turn, led to his conceiving and executing Il Fornaio's first restaurant in Corte Madera.

With characteristic exuberance, Stanley—one of Larry's biggest fans—explained, "Howard gets the credit, and rightly so. But deep down, part of me believes that Larry taught Howard a lot about how to be a great restaurant designer."

A bold statement with which Larry, who never took a design class in his life, would likely disagree. But it certainly points to a key part of his being.

As Marsha Guerrero concurred, "Larry is an artist."

An athlete all his life—still working out at the Bay Club into his late eighties—like many, although Larry really loved to win, he might have hated losing even more. Fighting like mad not to lose drove him.

Not surprisingly, in the run-up to the Corte Madera opening, he told the *Chronicle* that he "did not sleep for a week" prior to day one. "This one I was truly scared about. I hadn't hands-on opened a restaurant myself since 1983. Maybe I didn't know how to do it anymore. It seemed as if all my seventeen years in the business were on the line. I had nothing to fall back on. I had to make it, or I felt a good part of the reputation was down the tube."

Gino did his part, posting this message on his North Beach gas station's billboard:

> WE ARE BACK
> LARRY
> FRANCO
> JOE
> CLAUDIO
> STANLEY
> OCT 14
> IN MARIN

All that drive and attention to detail—never mind insomnia and artistry—paid off in Corte Madera. The restaurant opened in October 1987, just before Larry's fiftieth birthday. Patricia Unterman wrote a glowing review for the *Chronicle*, under the headline, "Marin Has the Real Thing for Italian Food Lovers." Her opening paragraph continued:

> Larry Mindel, the mastermind behind the wildly successful Spectrum chain of restaurants (Ciao, Prego, MacArthur Park) now owned by another group, has started a new venture. He bought the foundering Il Fornaio bakery chain and opened a flagship restaurant in one of them in Marin County. It's terrific.

If the concept was not yet indisputably proven in Corte Madera, it was off to a great start, showing legitimate promise. With Larry due to come off patent the following year—the non-compete expired fall of 1988—he could open in more lucrative locations.

San Francisco was the most logical spot for the next Il Fornaio restaurant. It was home, both literally and, more figuratively, to Larry's past business successes at Caswell and Spectrum. He knew from experience that San Francisco could be a very rewarding market.

He settled on a spot just a few blocks from Ciao and MacArthur Park: Levi's Plaza, completed in 1981 and described by the San Francisco Business Times as "the only true corporate campus in San Francisco." It housed the headquarters of Levi Strauss & Co., the longtime

San Francisco blue jeans manufacturer. Many other firms leased space in the 750,000 square foot office complex as well—diners just waiting to eat.

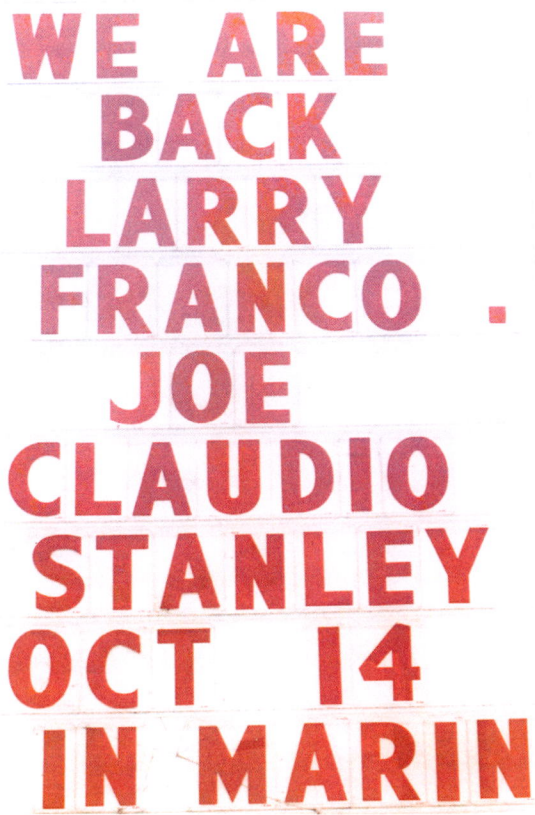

North Beach street cred

The campus was laid out thoughtfully, an "oasis on the Embarcadero" adjacent to Jackson Square, North Beach, and Telegraph Hill, its guiding aesthetic the idea of a "well-worn pair of blue jeans." Levi's newer red-brick buildings blended nicely with the area's historic warehouses. Much of the complex's space was dedicated to open plazas and parkland, designed by noted landscape architect Lawrence Halprin.

Early in 1988 the Chronicle's Ruthe Stein wrote a lengthy feature on Larry for the paper's People section. The piece doubled as a public announcement of Il Fornaio's intent to open at Levi's. A playful copy editor had a lot of fun: the story ran under a full-page headline hailing the "Resurrection of a Restaurateur," while a pull quote beneath proclaimed "Even exiled in a mall, he's still got the touch." Photos of several Spectrum San Francisco outlets including MacArthur Park and Ciao ran under the subhead, "A San Francisco Menu Mogul's Lost Empire."

Wanting to recruit the very best general manager he could find for Levi's, Larry flew to Los Angeles and asked onetime Chianti general manager and current Spectrum director of Southern California operations, Umberto Gibin—who originally started at Ciao—to leave "Anwar's Army" and join the growing number of former Spectrum people at Il Fornaio.

Umberto was very much in love with girlfriend Leslie Levine. Explaining why it took him so long to ask Leslie out on their first date, in 2011 Umberto jokingly told *SFGATE*, "I thought I wasn't good enough for her. I was just an Italian desperado."

Umberto wanted to accept Larry's offer. When he told Leslie about it, she said, "That sounds wonderful. And I will move to San Francisco with you—if you make an honest woman of me."

Duly nudged, Umberto proposed shortly thereafter. Leslie accepted, and Larry soon had the general manager he so strongly desired for Levi's.

Corte Madera's early success encouraged Larry, emboldening him to aim a little higher in San Francisco. Il Fornaio at Levi's footprint would be almost 40 percent larger than Corte Madera's—7,800 square feet to 5,600. The restaurant would officially be called Il Fornaio Gastronomia Italiana. "Gastronomia" was a wonderful catch-all word, suitably cosmopolitan but, more importantly, meant to convey Larry's vision of "a grand caffè and bar, bakery, pastry shop, pizzeria, and rosticceria wrapped up in one dazzling 'gastronomia italiana.'"

Umberto and his team opened Levi's in the fall of 1988, just after Larry's non-compete clause expired. The cuffs were finally off, and he came out swinging. The restaurant started strong, gained momentum, and within a year it was the subject of a rapturous review in Gourmet magazine, the national bible of fine dining.

Caroline Bates opened by writing, "San Francisco is a great place to visit, but I've never wanted to live here. Never, that is, until Larry Mindel unveiled Il Fornaio in Levi's Plaza…With such enticing food to eat in or take out, I figure that if I had an apartment nearby my entire day could be planned around Il Fornaio, or there would be no need or desire to eat anywhere else."

Bates described the ambience beautifully as she went on to write about her imaginary day as a nearby resident and patron:

> I'd eat a leisurely breakfast in the main dining room with the soothing sounds of Vivaldi on tape and beautiful objects all around me—majolica vases and pitchers from Umbria, flower sprays and fruit bowls on marble tables with exquisite wrought-iron bases in a grape-cluster design, and so much grey marble (wainscoting and table tops) that I wonder what the marble cutters of Massa and Carrara now do for a living. The room is magical at certain times, when daylight streams through the great arched windows, warming the yellow- and rust-washed walls…The windows frame a pretty glassed-in patio on the plaza and a backdrop of flowers and olive trees. 'Larry Mindel,' said an early press release, 'has transformed a block of San Francisco into a corner of Italy.' Well, he really has.

The pace quickened. Even before Levi's opened, construction was already underway on the third Il Fornaio restaurant in Del Mar (North County, San Diego).

Larry had a track record by now, both with Spectrum and with Il Fornaio in Corte Madera. Developers and landlords—people who owned commercial space—wanted successful or promising companies like Il Fornaio, headed by capable leaders like Larry, to occupy their buildings. The more money a tenant made, the more money the landlord would make. Success usually attracts or begets success. Sometimes all it takes is one: if a developer can bring in a strong tenant with a good reputation to anchor a commercial space, dominoes begin to fall. Other possible tenants want to be there, too, believing it will be a vibrant, profitable location.

Ivan Gayler, who, along with his partner David Winkler, was developing the Del Mar Plaza, called Larry several times, asking him to come look at their project. At first Larry politely declined. If he was going to do a restaurant that far from the Bay Area, it would be in Los Angeles, an area where he had already charted solid success. But Gayler was low-key persistent, and something in his phone voice and energy appealed to Larry. After Ivan's third or fourth call, Larry agreed to extend a bit farther south an already-scheduled trip to Los Angeles.

The two men met at the plaza, which was under construction. Ivan greeted Larry warmly and quickly led him up a small hill to a tree.

"Go ahead, climb up," Ivan suggested, pointing to the ladder that leaned against the tree and to a platform ten or twelve feet overhead. Larry looked at Ivan skeptically.

"What you see from the platform will be the exact view your guests enjoy. I think you should see it."

Ever-competitive Larry, in his standard dapper business attire, accepted the younger man's challenge and clambered up. Although he knew what to expect—he would be looking out at the Pacific Ocean—nonetheless his heart leapt when he made it to the platform and gazed west. The view was magnificent.

Larry took a moment to compose himself before descending the ladder, wanting to maintain at least some semblance of a poker face when he rejoined Ivan. The ocean view had all but sealed the transaction, but by this point in his career Larry knew the benefits of situational inscrutability. He still had a negotiation to conduct.

He told Ivan he was interested, but that he would need to think hard about Del Mar's distance from Il Fornaio headquarters in San Francisco and its low-density, non-metropolitan demographic. (Basic market research would soon reveal that the latter would not be problem: households within a five-mile radius boasted the state's highest income at that time, even higher than Beverly Hills.) Larry promised to be back in touch soon.

When he returned to San Francisco and discussed the Del Mar possibility with his associates—Franco, Umberto, Stanley, Valerie, and Ed—he shared one significant misgiving. He didn't want to move to Del Mar, and he felt as though it were asking a lot for anyone else to pull up stakes for the six months of supervision the build-out would require. His gut said they should not do the deal—would not, could not—unless someone Larry knew well and trusted greatly was on-site in Del Mar.

"I'll go," Stanley volunteered.

Larry was pleasantly surprised.

"Six months isn't that long. It'll be an experience, then I'll move back."

That obstacle surmounted, Larry focused on getting the best deal he could for the company. The lease was one part of that. How much would Il Fornaio pay building owner Ivan? This was pretty straightforward. There would be monthly rent, and then a break point: Il Fornaio would also pay Ivan somewhere from three to five percent on revenues if the restaurant did well and earnings exceeded a predetermined amount in a given month.

Build-out was the other part of the lease. There was more room to negotiate here. A build-out includes all interior and exterior finishes. A restaurateur starts with the very basic shell of a building, then turns it into an appealing space by way of paint, art, sound, lighting, woodwork, and stonework.

Developers like restaurants, risky though they are (90 percent fail within the first three years). As Jim Rosenfield, owner of the Marin Country Mart, rightly pointed out, "We all have to eat three times a day." People regularly consume many of those meals in restaurants, especially in affluent places like Marin and Del Mar. The steady flow of customers in those places is not only good for culinary tenants, but it also generates beneficial foot traffic for *all* of the shops in a specialty center. In an age when shoppers can get pretty much anything online, that's even more important for brick-and-mortar destinations.

Though risk-aware landlords want restaurants, ideally they look for ones owned and run by capable operators with a track record, people like Larry, who hit far more often than they miss. To attract them, developers sometimes pay a good portion of build-out costs.

Ivan wanted Il Fornaio in the Del Mar Plaza. He thought it would be the perfect centerpiece restaurant for his one-of-a-kind, casually upscale "European retail village," with its bougainvillea, fountains, Craftsman-style redwood pergola, and vast upper plaza looking out over the Pacific. Likewise, Larry wanted Il Fornaio in Del Mar, so long as the deal made sense, which in this case meant a generous allowance for improvements.

Each man liked and recognized something of himself in the other, realizing that theirs could be a very symbiotic partnership. They reached an agreement that would prove extremely beneficial for both sides.

Even before the deal was signed, Larry sent Stanley to Del Mar to scout further the location and conduct a more in-depth market analysis.

"Stanley, find out if they're ready for us down there. Is it really the right place for us to be?" was his charge to the thirty-three-year-old. He added that Stanley should be sure to wear his Armani suit, rent a nice car, and stay in a five-star hotel.

"Look the part. Have a great address and a great ride. This is a multi-million-dollar deal. Play the role, act like you deserve a potential landlord's attention and money."

When recalling the episode later, Stanley acknowledged that Larry's direction might sound superficial out of context. Not to him at the time. To the contrary, he heard and felt resonant authenticity in his boss's order, the subtext of which was essentially: *This is who we are, first cabin all the way. Be humble, treat people well—as you always do—but don't ever dumb down or apologize for our greatness. Own it.*

After Larry officially decided to proceed, Stanley moved south, into an apartment near Del Mar Plaza. He was busy from the start. Acting as Il Fornaio's always-available point person, he tracked construction, developed relationships in the community, and recruited and trained management and staff. The responsibility was daunting, but he thrived on the adrenaline and sense of accomplishment while things came together. As much as he had ever wanted anything in his work life, he wanted to justify the faith Larry had placed in him.

In the two months before opening, several other Il Fornaio people went down from San Francisco to help, including Franco and Marsha. Lino Chini, Del Mar's first general manager, was there, too. Larry was thrilled to have wooed Lino away from Chianti. Not only was he superb at his job, but hiring him was another satisfying loss for Spectrum and win for Il Fornaio.

Everyone lived in a hotel and "we worked our asses off," Marsha recalled. She and Stanley both felt a dramatic and suspenseful excitement and anxiety, similar to what a Broadway musical cast might experience as they ready for opening night. The schedule was demanding, the first-service deadline unyielding. But there were also occasional off-hours respites, which sanity required.

On opening night Larry himself experienced a double dose of suspense. He was uncharacteristically late to the event, dallying in his hotel room. As he donned his tuxedo and dabbed his cologne, he also hollered at the television, rooting hard for his beloved Michigan Wolverines to win their first—and so far only—NCAA basketball national championship.

It was a tight, overtime game. Larry was elated and relieved when Michigan finally won. But a new wave of uncertainty surged through him as he walked the two blocks to the restaurant. *How would Il Fornaio play south of the Grapevine?*, a reference to the stretch of I-5 north of Los Angeles and long considered the practical boundary between Northern and Southern California.

When he rounded the corner to the restaurant, he saw more than 100 diners lined up on the sidewalk, waiting for their first meal at the new restaurant. Two wins in one night!

Il Fornaio Del Mar burst from the gate and never looked back. It remains a steady performer today. Its success was pivotal to the company's growth, since it proved—to Larry and his team, as well to future investors—that Il Fornaio had the ability to prosper in a different market far from home. This was key to any expansion hopes.

Shortly after Del Mar's debut, everyone in the corporate opening crew—except Lino—returned to San Francisco. Not to rest, but to get back at it. The fourth Il Fornaio, in Palo Alto, was scheduled to open in late October. Soon everyone was energized, operating in positive frenzy mode once again.

The restaurant would be located in the Garden Court Hotel, which had opened in downtown Palo Alto just three years before, in 1986. An outside company originally operated the hotel's restaurant, catering, and room service. The hotel owners were not satisfied with the operator's performance.

Larry was familiar with downtown Palo Alto because one of the original Il Fornaio bakeries, already open when he took over in 1987, was located on University Avenue. The bakery did well—in contrast to most of the others—which opened Larry's eyes to the area's potential.

When Norm Rosenblatt of the Garden Court wondered if Il Fornaio might want to take over the hotel's restaurant, in addition to its catering and room service, Larry thought the opportunity merited serious consideration. One thing led to another, negotiations ensued, and soon work was underway in Palo Alto.

On October 17, just minutes before the San Francisco Giants were set to host the Oakland A's in Game 3 of the World Series at Candlestick Park, the Loma Prieta earthquake hit. Sixty-three people died, and 27,000 structures were damaged—from the Bay Bridge and the Embarcadero Freeway to smaller structures in the Marina, including Mimi's house.

The day after the quake, with "normal" life in Northern California inconceivable for the immediate future, Larry piled several associates into his car and drove from San Francisco to Palo Alto. It was no easy journey. Power was off in most places. Many streets, bridges, and freeways were closed. But Larry was determined to get the group to Palo Alto. He wanted boots on the ground, since the restaurant was set to open the following week.

At first Larry didn't even know about the quake. He was in Palo Alto, driving to a record store to purchase CDs for the restaurant. He was surprised to find the store's front door locked before closing time. After banging on it without success, he tried around back. An employee explained there had just been an earthquake.

"Oh, okay," said Larry, unaware of its severity. "But I've still got a restaurant to open. I just need a few CDs. I'll be in and out quickly."

"I don't think you understand," the clerk retorted. "This wasn't a routine little quake. Everything's everywhere. Our stock is all over the floor. We're not open. Go away!"

When Larry's group made it to Palo Alto the day after, they were relieved to find no real structural damage to the hotel and that the gas lines were still intact—not the case in many places. They were still on track to open as planned.

There were, however, some relatively minor cosmetic challenges. Mirrors fell from the walls, replacements for which would not arrive for weeks. Signage explaining "Mirrors will go here" was painted in tasteful script, so that early diners could visualize how the completed restaurant would look.

"The signs weren't corny or tacky, of course," Marsha explained. "Everything Larry did was tasteful."

The earthquake was devastating to many, but two small silver linings emerged from the disaster.

First, people's perspective changed overnight. Customers, vendors, staff: everyone was more patient and understanding, weathering any opening issues with more grace than they might have in normal circumstances.

Second, Il Fornaio showed people in the Palo Alto area that they could get a San Francisco big-city dining experience without leaving home. It took months for San Francisco to fully recover from the quake, long enough for some in the South Bay to develop new dining-out habits. Il Fornaio Palo Alto was a beneficiary of this shift, the right restaurant in the right place at the right time.

This "rightness" only grew over time, as technology and venture capital became bigger forces in the American economy. Suddenly, Silicon Valley was *the* place to be for ambitious, disruptive fortune seekers. Il Fornaio Palo Alto emerged as the Valley's apex restaurant and meeting spot.

Scores of tech and venture-capital titans ate there, including Steve Jobs. Though not necessarily a staff favorite—he could be prickly and tight with a buck, not to mention with his deodorant—he always sat in booth 57.

In his best-selling Jobs biography, Walter Isaacson wrote, "One day Reed Jobs (Steve's son) was discussing with his family where to take his girlfriend for dinner. His father suggested Il Fornaio, an elegant standard in Palo Alto, but Reed said he had been unable to get reservations. 'Do you want me to try?' his father asked. Reed resisted; he wanted to handle it himself."

President Clinton's daughter Chelsea would come with her Secret Service security detail when she was a student at Stanford, as would the school's provost, Condoleezza Rice, in the years before she left for Washington to serve as George W. Bush's secretary of state. U2 front man and activist Bono ate there occasionally. Many 49er football players—including Joe Montana, Ronnie Lott, and Harris Barton, as well as Steve Young—still drop in today.

The Washington Post published a "Geek Guide to Silicon Valley," which listed twelve must-see spots for those planning a pilgrimage. Destinations included Stanford University, Apple Computer, Intel Corporation, and—right there amidst those hugely iconic and influential venues—Il Fornaio Palo Alto.

Branching Out

In April of 1990 Larry and the team opened what he told the *San Francisco Chronicle* would be his "most ambitious project yet," Etrusca.

He loved the Il Fornaios, all four thriving. Yet for all their beautiful interiors and superb service, in his mind they were still trattorias: traditionally family-owned, casual neighborhood restaurants found throughout Italy and serving fresh, unassuming but delicious local food. Even as he intended to open many more Il Fornaios, part of Larry also yearned to open a true Italian *ristorante* in the city—ristorantes being more formal and sophisticated than trattorias.

"It was always going to be a one-off," he explained. "I wanted it to be the finest Italian ristorante in San Francisco."

Spectrum Foods ultimately grew to feature several quite different concepts—to name a few, Chianti, Ciao, and Prego were Italian; MacArthur Park was American; Guaymus was Mexican—all under the umbrella of one parent company.

Steeped as he was in that innovative Spectrum experience, to Larry Etrusca felt like the logical next step for him and Il Fornaio. As Patricia Unterman explained in her June 3, 1990, *Chronicle* review, Etrusca was "meant to satisfy slightly higher, more luxurious and more expensive dining-out tastes than Il Fornaio."

Larry and his Il Fornaio associates spent three years researching "the fun-food-and-wine-loving" Etruscans who occupied west-central Italy 3,000 years ago.

Speaking with the *Chronicle's* "People In Business" columnist Lloyd Watson, Larry quipped, "The Etruscans were the original party animals."

Part of the group's research included a trip—of course!—to the ancient thermal baths at Saturnia. Believed by the Etruscans to be a gift from the gods, Larry and the team took the healing waters.

Once back in San Francisco, they directed their attention to another site rich in history: Rincon Center. Originally owned by the Southern Pacific Railroad and later home to a United States Mail sorting center, the building occupied an entire block south of Market. Bounded by Mission, Spear, Howard, and Steuart Streets, it was a three-minute walk from Caswell Coffee, where it all started for Larry.

As was the case in Del Mar, at Rincon Larry was "on the developer's radar." The developer approached him with a very attractive offer. The tenant improvement allowance (TIA), money a developer spends to customize a space to a tenant's specifications, was phenomenal.

"He basically put it on a silver platter for us," Larry said.

Success bred success for Larry, despite his being in an industry generally regarded as fickle and risky. Rather than trying to find a viable location, then convince a landlord to take a chance on him and his business, owners were now coming to Larry, offering favorable terms.

The team conceived a ristorante worthy of the space, as Unterman attested when she wrote, "The designers have outdone themselves in creating a stunning, large-scale dining room resplendent with polished bird's-eye maple and oxblood mahogany, white marble, onyx and yards of hand-painted frescoes."

Not that construction was without its obstacles and frustrations—like with almost all of Larry's restaurants.

With site work effectively complete, an opening date set, and employees scheduled to work, a city inspection revealed that the space behind the bar was six inches narrower than code; it would not allow for easy wheelchair access. The contractor spent two weeks tearing out the beautiful, expensive bar and building a new one six inches the other direction. Etrusca never employed a wheelchair-using bartender, but they could have.

In the end, Larry hit his intended mark. As Unterman wrote in her review:

> A dinner at Etrusca can present a real night out—it's worth dressing up for. The magical lighting at this restaurant makes everyone look like an Armani-clad character in a reminiscence by Fellini. It is easy to imagine yourself in some resonant restaurant in Rome, as the meal unfolds to the rhythm of the kitchen.

You don't feel hurried here, so you are tempted to order three or four courses like the Italians do. You can actually talk, discreetly seated in high-sided booths upholstered in glove leather, while sipping luscious, regional Italian wines.

In the "People in Business" piece, Watson cited numbers as he broke news of the coming Etrusca. He said at that time (March 1990), "the average U.S. restaurant does $150 in sales per square foot, with a good dinner house doing about double that. Mindel's four Il Fornaio restaurants—in Levi's Plaza, Corte Madera, Palo Alto and Del Mar—have been topping $750 a square foot."

Not long after Etrusca opened, Larry's son Michael joined Il Fornaio. Michael graduated from Cal in 1986, and then, with no background in journalism, moved to Chicago and began work as assistant to the editor of the *Daily Market Digest*, an afternoon business paper owned by Larry Levy, Michael's dad's YPO friend and fellow restaurateur.

Michael's brave move to the Windy City forced him to establish himself in a place where he knew no one. His first job exposed him to many different areas of business. Both father and son believe that it was helpful, maybe even crucial, for Michael to begin his business career working for someone other than his father.

In addition to owning the paper for which Michael wrote, Larry Levy was a serial entrepreneur who, along with his brother Mark, built Levy Restaurants from a single delicatessen in Chicago to the largest provider of sports and entertainment catering in the country, serving a long list of well-known clients, including Wrigley Field; Barclays in Brooklyn; Allegiant in Las Vegas; Staples (now Crypto) in Los Angeles; Ford Field in Detroit, and Churchill Downs. Levy also founded Cresset Real Estate Partners, as well as being one of Chicago's most active angel investors. He and his sons manage Levy Family Partners, owning significant stakes in Del Taco Restaurants, Nest, Peloton, SpaceX, and the Esperanza Resort in Cabo San Lucas.

When asked what advice he would give his twenty-eight-year-old self, Levy replied, "It may sound cliché, but it's true: know your passions. Mine happen to be sports, food, and rock and roll. What happens in stadiums? All those things. I'm incredibly fortunate to have built a business that aligns so well with my passions. I would tell any young entrepreneur to really explore what they care about and stick with their passions."

In that same interview, Levy said, "Never work for someone you don't respect. I don't care how much money they offer or how great the title. Walk away right away. Life's too short to work for someone, or an organization, that doesn't value you and treat you as you deserve to be treated. That should be non-negotiable for anyone."

Levy currently sits on the boards of the Art Institute of Chicago, the Lincoln Park Zoo, Northwestern University, and the Kellogg Graduate School of Management.

Michael could have done much worse for a first boss.

Michael returned to the Bay in October 1988, working as an account executive for Chiat/Day, a cutting-edge advertising agency servicing notable clients, such as 3Com and Sutter Home Winery. Their California Cooler "The Real Stuff" campaign—specifically 1986's "The Chairman" spot, set to Spencer Davis's "Gimme Some Lovin'"—still shines.

Not quite two years later, Michael was staying on the third floor of his parents' home in Sausalito, recovering from back surgery. A three-sport standout at Branson and a defenseman on Cal's club lacrosse team, he had to undergo a pressure-relieving procedure on a herniated disk, unusual for someone so young.

Larry climbed the stairs each night to check on Michael during that weeklong convalescence. One evening he asked, "How's your job, son? How are you liking it? What about advertising in general, how are you liking that? What are your goals? Where do you see yourself in five years?"

It was a little much for Michael, floating as he was in something of a Vicodin haze.

Michael understood Larry clearly enough, though, when he suggested he might retire within the next five years.

As Michael lay in bed over the next several days, continuing to recover, he pondered Larry's questions, as well as the reality that the window for him to work alongside his father would not stay open forever.

When Michael asked himself the same questions Larry had asked, he realized he wasn't all that enamored with advertising. It had been fun at first, but when he looked down the road, he didn't like the quality of life. He saw too much pressure, too many destructive tendencies and not enough sanity. Blazing his own trail in industries other than restaurants had been important to him out of college, but he had met that challenge. Now, he realized, he kind of *missed* restaurants.

He approached Larry and asked, "What would you think if I came to work at Il Fornaio?"

"That might work," Larry replied. "I know they need a waiter in Corte Madera."

This was hardly what Michael had envisioned. He would later admit to having had "delusions of grandeur," assuming he would slide in as director, if not vice president of marketing.

Sleeping on his father's "offer," he woke up realizing that working as server made sense. Someday he hoped to work at a higher level in the company. Learning the business from the ground up would serve him well, if and when he climbed the Il Fornaio ladder.

What's more, Michael guessed that waiting tables would be something of a respite from the Chiat/Day grind, with its 7:00 a.m. client meetings and late-night pitch-preparation sessions. Recalling that a physical therapist had suggested "motion might be the lotion," Michael suspected that a server's five hours of fast-paced movement would be better for his back than nine hours anchored to a desk.

He also knew Il Fornaio was "really beginning to roll." If he accepted Larry's invitation, he would likely be joining a long-term winner—an appealing prospect. Eager to see if a restaurant career was right for him, and whether working with Larry would be right for them both, Michael joined the company in September 1990.

He quickly realized two things.

One, a server's job is considerably more complicated than it might look to the untrained eye. Two, for him the work was really fun—he liked it more than he thought he would.

More often than not, Michael got to make people happy. He had been on teams all his life. He knew the joy of playing a specific role on a great one. As a server, his role was to be an intelligent and convivial conduit, guiding patrons through the menu and wine list, then returning to the table bearing his teammates' delicious creations and selections.

Michael believed in the product to his core, not just because it was his dad's restaurant, but because he knew—all bias aside—that Il Fornaio's food, ambience, and service were first-rate. This made the work "easy" and fun. Leaving at shift's end with a nice wad in his pocket and no further responsibilities was a welcome change for Michael. In retrospect, he considered the lifestyle "awesome."

After eighteen relatively carefree months as a waiter, Michael joined Il Fornaio's new Manager Training Program, something director of operations Mark Walker put together. Mark knew the company would only continue to grow and, therefore, needed a consistent supply of managerial talent.

Once Michael completed the eight-week program, he was sent to Il Fornaio Levi's Plaza in San Francisco as an assistant manager. By 1995 he was Il Fornaio's director of marketing. In 1998 he became the company's marketing vice president.

Michael wasn't the only one who liked working for Larry at Il Fornaio. Dishwashers, food-prep people, busboys, waiters, chefs, and managers all felt seen, respected, supported, and well-compensated.

Jonathan Sigal, a personable, if—by his own admission—sometimes scattered server, worked at the Corte Madera restaurant in the early 1990s. Prior to joining Il Fornaio, his professional experiences led him and his wife, Mary, to believe that having a child in the Bay Area was a "luxury" beyond their means. Il Fornaio's strong health plan, which Jon characterized as "unheard of elsewhere at the time," gave them the hope and wherewithal to take the parental plunge. Today their son Ari, the absolute apple of his grateful father's eye, is a thirty-five-year-old Redwood and Cal grad turned top tech executive.

Jon is no outlier. For years Il Fornaio's employee turnover rate was well below industry average, with many people working more than ten years for the company. Some worked as long as twenty-five.

Hourly workers at Il Fornaio did well. Chefs and managers did even better through the company's partnership program, which offered stock options to encourage commitment to the restaurants' long-term success.

Larry's mission was to provide customers with "the most authentic Italian experience outside of Italy." One fun and effective way to ensure this was to take ten different managers and chefs each year on a two-week trip to Italy, immersing them in its food, wine, culture, and lifestyle. It was quite a perk.

At the same time Michael joined Il Fornaio, Larry bought land and an old cabin in Montana's Bitterroot Valley, along with partners Tom Hyde, Bob Coleman, and Bob Cantor. Though Cantor would sell his share early on, Larry, Tom, and Bob Coleman remain partners today.

The group agreed that Howard Backen, the architect who designed the remodel of Larry's Sausalito house, as well as all the Il Fornaio restaurants up to that date, would oversee renovation and expansion of the cabin on Flagger Lane.

One publication called Backen "a rustic architect to the stars." He worked with winemakers Tim Mondavi and Bill Harlan; Apple's Steve Jobs; DreamWorks head Jeffrey Katzenberg; Robert Redford; and director Nancy Meyers, who paid Howard tribute by decorating the architect's office in her Steve Martin movie *It's Complicated* with photos of Backen-designed buildings.

Howard did a magnificent job on the sprawling lodgepole-pine log home, including nonsensical light switches, a quirk Larry attributes to passion.

Howard and his interior designer, Lori O'Kane, fell in love while working on the project. If some practical details such as where to most intelligently place a light switch got away from the pair, romantics accepted it with a smile. They believe that Howard and Lori's love, though not enduring—they married and divorced—still imbues the lodge with a special spirit.

For more than thirty years, Larry has spent an entire month each summer at the special retreat, masterfully balancing the right amount of fulfilling remote work with fishing, fishing, and more fishing.

Well into Larry's sixties, summer dinners at Flagger Lane didn't commence until twilight's end at 10:00 p.m. There were fish to catch, showers to savor, clothes to don just so, and cocktails to mix and enjoy. And there was always family, Larry's bliss, one set of children and grandchildren arriving just as another departed.

Larry hosted several Il Fornaio senior staff retreats in Montana. One fall trip Marsha and Stanley were "relegated" to the screened-in sleeping porch, Larry explaining apologetically to the late-arrivers that other staff had already claimed the interior beds.

"As it turned out, we didn't feel relegated at all," Marsha reminisced. "We were like middle-aged kids. The nights were brisk, but the quilts were warm. It was wonderful!"

Larry with daughter Katherine at Ravalli County Fair; Hamilton, Montana, 2007

A 2025 human resources professional might question some of the old retreat norms, such as a woman showing up for breakfast meetings in her bathrobe. But times were different.

Besides, Marsha pointed out, "We got a lot of good work done on those trips."

Larry agreed, adding that he also did some of his best work *solo* in Montana. His one-man stints were rarely intentional, more often than not happening at the beginning or end of trips that included guests. Still, at least once he returned to California after a few days alone in the Bitterroot feeling calm and confident, the solution to a vexing business problem now clear in his mind and heart.

Perhaps time in Montana helped crystallize Larry's vision for his follow-up to Etrusca: Il Fornaio Irvine, which opened in late 1991.

As with Del Mar and Rincon Center, a development company really wanted Il Fornaio to occupy its space just off the 405 freeway, minutes from John Wayne Airport in Orange County. They threw in all sorts of incentives, including not one but two bocce courts. (This was twenty years before bocce became the rage in the U.S. and Bar Bocce opened in Sausalito.). They upped the ante with multiple private dining rooms and a rotunda with a retractable roof.

Today Il Fornaio Irvine continues to amaze. In its initial review on January 2, 1992, the *Los Angeles Times* called the restaurant, "stunning…it may be the flashiest restaurant ever to open in Orange County," and estimated that, between them, Il Fornaio and the developer put almost $4 million into the showplace.

Prego Irvine, Spectrum Foods' signature outpost just a few doors down across Von Karman Avenue, had been thriving for five years. Only an extremely confident man would open an Il Fornaio steps away. Larry was far more focused on the developer's incredible near-"blank check" deal than he was on the opportunity to compete directly against a Spectrum outlet.

> "It ain't bragging if you can do it."
>
> —Dizzy Dean, St. Louis Cardinal pitcher

Etrusca and Il Fornaio Irvine were just two examples of Larry's unfaltering ability to secure extremely favorable leases and tenant improvement allowances for his restaurants, giving him a reputation as an outstanding negotiator. One of his personal credos: *don't ever own the building, always lease.* And don't personally guarantee a lease either; pouring a million dollars into improvements is guarantee enough.

When an interviewer asked if there was a secret to Larry's negotiating success, she expected banter along the lines of *landlords as partners, everyone in it together, a rising tide lifting all boats, win-win negotiating,* and *finding solutions that work for everyone.*

"I'm not looking for fair," Larry responded instead. "The restaurant business is tough. I want to make money. I don't give a shit what's fair. I want to win."

His tone wasn't belligerent, but rather light, even playful. It was that of a man extremely secure and comfortable in his own skin. A man who isn't afraid.

Larry had heard about the new-school collaborative approach to negotiating.

"That's ridiculous!" he concluded. "I'm out to win, and I don't care who knows it. I assume the other guy wants to win, too. Nothing wrong with that. Game on!"

One of Larry's negotiating secret weapons was his disposition. He shot straight. He was honest, authentic, reasonable, and friendly. Even if a person disagreed with his argument, it was hard not to enjoy and respect the man himself—if not indulge some of his smaller, well-known quirks, such as his refusal to pay common area maintenance charges because "*I just don't do it.*"

Larry knew exactly who he and his associates were and what they could accomplish. It was the purest form of leverage. No bluster necessary.

Il Fornaio Forges Forward

In 1992 the Beverly Hills Il Fornaio bakery, open at that same spot since 1981, expanded into a full-service restaurant. For years the entertainment industry power-breakfast spot had "secretly" served select customers eggs cooked on a hidden hot plate—unbeknownst to the health department.

Il Fornaio Beverly Hills soon became to Hollywood what Il Fornaio Palo Alto had already become to Silicon Valley. The company was now a cultural phenomenon.

Il Fornaio San Jose also opened in 1992. The restaurant was located in the historic Sainte Claire Hotel, which had just been redone by Manou Mobedshahi. His fifteen-room Sherman House in San Francisco was, according to the *San Francisco Chronicle*, "considered one of the world's grande luxe hostelries." Manou fell in love with the Sainte Claire's elegant façade and spacious public rooms on first sight.

As part of a hotel, Il Fornaio San Jose presented several logistical challenges, from twenty-four-hour room service and banquet catering, to dining rooms and kitchens on different floors. As always, he and the team found ways to meet those challenges—even when work and life collided.

Stanley, who had been part of the critical opening team at many Il Fornaios, was stretched to the breaking point at San Jose. His father was dying as the restaurant was opening. Ever the professional, Stanley pressed on.

Il Fornaio Pasadena opened in 1992, and Il Fornaio Sacramento opened in 1993. Though no one consciously strove for this particular distinction or embraced it in real time, Sacramento marked a significant milestone in the company's growth. Looking back, all agree it was evidence of maturation.

The head chef disappeared the week before opening night, a hectic and crucial stretch of eighteen-hour days—teaching staff, taking deliveries, working out kinks—that can determine a restaurant's fate. Larry had no idea.

He had decided to boat to the opening. For the day or two it took him to meander up the delta to Sacramento, he was out of touch. Cell phones were just coming into vogue, and service and coverage were rudimentary. There were periods in the delta backwaters when he could not be reached.

Larry would never have felt comfortable boating to an earlier opening. On some level he must have now realized he had created a company that could handle the craziness of, say, a key member of staff disappearing at a critical time.

Other team members stepped up, and by the time Larry docked in Sacramento, everything was on track. The restaurant opened successfully and is still thriving today, boosted later by its proximity to the Sacramento Kings's Golden 1 Arena, which opened two blocks away in 2016.

Stanford MBA Ed Levine had been Il Fornaio's chief financial officer from the time Larry acquired the company. The nature of their respective roles meant that Larry and Ed would sometimes clash. One staffer said it was Larry the Dreamer versus Ed the Bean Counter, marble versus Formica.

Larry believed the company had to spend money to make money; Ed thought they should be more fiscally conservative. He didn't believe in spending $350 a square foot on build-out when $250 would do.

Ed left in 1992 to become chief executive officer of Gordon Biersch Brewing Company. Not long after, he partnered with Roland Passot to create several Left Bank brasseries, including the mother ship on Magnolia in Larkspur, California.

After Ed left, Larry brought in longtime Spectrum stalwart Chuck Frank as a consultant. Chuck was president of Spectrum when Marriott bought Saga and Spectrum. He served out his contractual obligation to Marriott following the sale, primarily to ensure Spectrum chefs and managers got their promised rewards. As soon as that obligation was satisfied—on the very first day he legally could—Chuck left.

After a very brief "retirement"—his wife, Barbara, quickly fired him from that role, insisting, "You need to get out of the house!"—Chuck founded CAF Restaurant Services, Inc., a successful restaurant consulting firm. In addition to Il Fornaio, one of his first clients was Johnny Rockets. He took them from four stores to 100.

Chuck didn't consult at Il Fornaio long. Instead he became a full-time employee of the company, serving as president and chief operating officer.

The Mille

Around this time, two of Larry's central passions, cars and Italy, came together for seventy-two euphoric hours.

In May of 1992 Larry drove in the *Mille Miglia*. The Mille remains Italy's most famous road race, even though it was last contested as a true, all-out race in 1957. It has been featured in several movies, most recently 2023's *Ferrari*.

Mille Miglia means "one thousand miles." The race ran from Brescia to Rome and back to Brescia, taking place on public roads. The streets were closed to everyday traffic, but the high speeds, narrow lanes, and spectators crowding the route made it a dangerous and, far too often, deadly test. Over its thirty-year history, twenty-four drivers and navigators and thirty-two spectators died. Thirty-five of the fatalities occurred between 1948 and 1957, an average of almost four per race.

Stirling Moss, who in 1955 posted the Mille's fastest time ever—ten hours, seven minutes, and forty-eight seconds, almost 100 miles per hour—said, "The roads were really quite narrow. They estimate five million people saw the race, and spectators were a big problem, because if they were lining the inside of the corner, you couldn't see where you wanted to make your apex. They were literally on the side of the damned road. You couldn't see what the corner was like."

The government outlawed racing on public roads after 1957, when eleven people were killed at the village of Guidizzolo: Spanish driver Alfonso de Portago, American co-driver and navigator Edmund Nelson, and nine spectators, five of them children.

In 1977 the event came back to life as a regularity rally, a much safer multi-day automobile "parade" in which drivers are tested on how well they meet average time and speed requirements, usually in compliance with local laws. Participants must drive cars entered in the twenty-four Mille Miglias between 1927 and 1957.

Those wanting to drive in the event must apply; space is limited. Simply wanting to participate, disposing of the means, and having access to a qualified car is not enough. Demand outstrips supply.

A friend was willing to loan Larry an unspectacular Fiat that met rally specifications. Often a driver's car is his passport in. The race committee sees it on his application and says, "Yes! We want that rare and gorgeous 1953 Ferrari!"

No such chariot graced Larry's application. However, though his car may have been unexceptional, his distinction as the first American and person of non-Italian descent to receive the prestigious Caterina de Medici medal glittered. The race committee essentially conceded *the car is* niente di speciale, *but the driver—an American honored by the Italian government!—now there's a man! Application accepted!*

Larry received his Mille acceptance letter at work. He walked down the hall to *maestro* Franco Galli's office. When he showed his intended *co-piloto* (co-driver and navigator) the letter, Franco began to cry. He had grown up a big fan of the race, cheering the exotic cars as they passed through his hometown. The idea that he would now be in one of them himself moved him to tears.

The Mille was one of the peak experiences of Larry's life. Even the safe-and-sane, no-one-dies version of the event had him buzzing for weeks. Roaring along two-lane country roads. Downshifting through tiny villages whose cobblestone streets were packed with exuberant Italians whooping their approval. Fetching rural maidens offering warm "welcome to our municipality" hugs and kisses at every lunch and dinner. The car nut from Toledo felt he had died and gone to *paradiso*.

One of Larry's Bay Area friends, Martin Swig, an auto dealership magnate and collector whose uncle once owned the Fairmont Hotel chain, had driven in the Mille Miglia years before. Martin returned to Sausalito with the dream of creating a California Mille, something he mentioned frequently to Larry. Eventually, with Swig taking lead, the two men worked with others to create the California Mille, an annual four-day, thousand-mile car tour on public roads.

Inspired by the Italian regularity rally from which it takes its name, the California Mille is open to cars that either ran or would have been eligible to run in the original 1927-1957 Brescia-Rome-Brescia event. Fields typically include vintage Alfa Romeos, Ferraris, Mercedes-Benzes, and Porsches. The event's slogan is "Great Cars, Little Roads, and Wonderful Friends."

Promotional literature states, "The route changes each year, but consists of back roads through some of California's most scenic areas, including Highway 1 along Northern California's coast, Napa and Sonoma Valleys, and the Sierra Nevada. Each day is punctuated by several stops for meals and refreshments at significant wineries and restaurants, while overnight accommodation is generally at some of California's best hotels. A California Highway Patrol escort accompanies the group to facilitate traffic control and communications."

Il Fornaio was a natural corporate sponsor for the event. In its first years, the rally started and ended at Il Fornaio in Corte Madera. The parking lot was quite a sight: sixty-five gorgeous European classics all in one spot.

The Italian Mille will always top Larry's automotive list, but a close second was driving the California Mille in the late 1990s with his son Michael, who, as director of marketing, was an established member of the Il Fornaio corporate team by then. As such, the rally was "fun work" for the pair.

That year's route included a special foray onto a rural raceway where participants could safely—and legally—really open it up, to see what they and their cars could do. A photographer snapped a shot of Larry and Michael rocketing along the backstretch of that speedway in a borrowed 1950s Alfa Romeo convertible. An enlarged print still hangs, as it has for decades, in the hall outside the men's room at the Corte Madera Il Fornaio. Companion shots from Italian Milles hang nearby. The grouping is a simple cheat code to Larry's passions: Italy, cars, family.

Sometime in the early 2000s, Swig sold Larry a 1957 Lancia Aurelia. The car was old enough to qualify for both the Italian and American Milles, but Swig's pitch to Larry focused more on nationality than on age.

"Italy's your country, Larry, not Germany. You're an Italian restaurateur, not a German one. You should be driving an Italian classic, not a Porsche (a reference to the beautiful 356 Larry had at the time). A modern Porsche is fine for your daily beater, but for special days you need an Italian car."

Son Michael at the wheel, Larry *co-piloto*; California Mille; 1996.
Similar photo still hangs in the Corte Madera Il Fornaio restroom hallway.

Larry bought the car. Swig's 2012 obituary suggested there may have been more to the transaction than thoughtful friendship: "'When I found I had about forty vintage cars, I made a deal with my wife,' Swig loved to say. 'Each time I bought a new old car, I agreed to sell one. I'm running slightly behind on my half of the bargain.'"

Larry took delivery of the car at the California Mille that began at the Fairmont Hotel in San Francisco. He was excited, and the sights, sounds, and smells of the rally's start heightened his delight—delight that turned to anger when his new toy crapped out not five miles in, halfway across the Golden Gate Bridge. The car "came in on the hook," as mechanics say—it had to be towed to a garage. Larry took his fellow drivers' playful taunts in stride.

Repairs were made, and the car runs beautifully today.

Mixing Business with Pleasure

In 1993 Larry's daughter Laura married Steve, a friend of Michael's. Their brief engagement—he proposed and she accepted on February 4; they married on July 4—and at-home nuptials might seem quaint today, when extended run-ups and destination weddings are so common. But the bride has no regrets.

"It was perfect," Laura reminisced. "I still can't believe Dad and Debby were willing to take out all the furniture."

The party was very much an Il Fornaio wedding. Mother-of-the-bride Mimi's boyfriend, Herb Arnold, a successful New York real-estate entrepreneur and accomplished sculptor, was dying of cancer that spring. Mimi was often away and, understandably, preoccupied when home. Larry was busy opening Sacramento and Pasadena, and Debby had her hands full with young Katherine and Nick.

Laura and Debby met once with San Francisco's highest profile and most flamboyant event producer. It did not go well.

Larry told Laura not to worry. He would figure something out.

Several days later, Il Fornaio's "Swiss Army knife," Stanley Morris, was either assigned or volunteered to coordinate the event. It became a beautiful embodiment of Larry's blurred life-work mix.

According to Stanley's partner on the project, Marsha Guerrero, she and Stanley were neither assigned to wedding, nor did they volunteer. They were *invited* to work it.

"We were so proud to be invited," she said.

Larry's associates and workers were often his friends. Many of his friends were also his associates and workers. It was an inspiring interweave.

Technically Il Fornaio simply catered the party. In reality, Stanley acted as a full-blown wedding planner, writing up a comprehensive six-page Order of Events covering July 1–July 4. It included the rehearsal, seating charts, photo schedule, musicians, and processional, not to mention shepherding everyone through the proceedings with warmth, humor, and confidence. Laura did a lot, but Stanley and Marsha were indispensable.

Larry and Debby's kitchen was stretched to maximum capacity. Fifteen guests at Christmas was one thing; 220 for the wedding something else entirely.

"What Does A Father Say?" Larry and daughter Laura at her wedding; Sausalito, 1993

The food was Italian, of course. Larry's North Beach *paisan*, Gino Biradelli, added to the atmosphere by sending a tuxedoed trio right out of *The Godfather*—accordion player, guitarist, and violinist—to stroll the garden. He also sent a multi-flavored freezer cart from his *gelateria*. In keeping with the Italian theme, bride and groom vroomed off to the first night of their honeymoon in Larry's black Ferrari Mondial.

Although one hundred percent Laura's afternoon and evening, Larry stole the show with his epic "What Does A Father Say?" toast, which left few dry eyes. The new husband wondered if he had bitten off a bigger breadstick than he could chew, something compounded by the gift he and Laura received from Il Fornaio board member Pierre Mornell.

North Beach "mayor" Gino Biradelli sent strolling trio as wedding gift.

At first glance, Pierre might have appeared to be a slight outlier on Il Fornaio's formidable board of directors. Unlike the other board members, he was not a traditional executive. A renowned UCSF-trained psychiatrist, Mornell began his career as a Mill Valley marriage counselor before expanding into corporate consulting.

Pierre's background in conflict resolution was often a valuable asset, as was what Larry considered his "wisdom and maturity." Il Fornaio board members were as confident as they were accomplished in their respective industries. Two particular alpha males were frequently at loggerheads; Pierre helped channel energy that might otherwise have been detrimental into respectful, productive "creative tension."

He gave the couple two books he had written in his marriage-counseling days. The blurb on the cover of *Passive Men, Wild Women* promised "Timely. Controversial. Enlightening. A leading psychiatrist and marriage counselor tells you why women want more and men want less—and what you can do about it to save your relationship!"

Laura's spouse was surprised—his background was slightly more conventional than Laura's. In his world, serving platters or dessert plates were more typical wedding gifts.

The second book was even more provocative: *The Lovebook: What Works in a Lasting Sexual Relationship*.

Other board members at the wedding included investment banker Warren Hellman; Williams Sonoma, Pottery Barn, and West Elm CEO Howard Lester; venture capitalist Scott Hedrick; and Dreyer's Grand Ice Cream CEO—and Cal crew benefactor—Gary Rogers. Sadly, all of these men are gone now, as is Pierre.

Moving On

Opening San Jose and running Laura's wedding turned out to be Stanley's farewell.

When he said his final goodbye to his ailing father in October of 1992, he mentioned he might be moving on from Il Fornaio in the not-too-distant future. His father was surprised.

"Are you sure?" he asked. "This has been a really good twelve years for you."

Stanley knew himself and the company well enough to know it was time. The company was growing; he didn't like that he no longer knew everyone by name.

When he left in early 1994, Larry told him, "We're throwing you a going-away party, Stanley. We'll do it in San Jose at one of the private dining rooms in the hotel, black tie, fifty or sixty people, invite whomever you want." Stanley was touched.

He went on a remarkable run, serving as: vice-president of operations for Equinox Concepts, a company established to license, develop, and operate U.S. food and beverage concepts in Asia, for which he ran Stars restaurant and Spinelli Coffee in Singapore; general manager of Hapuku Lodge and Tree Houses, a small luxury hotel on New Zealand's South Island; managing partner of Teatro ZinZanni, San Francisco's legendary cirque nightclub venue; a similar role for a comparable setup in New Orleans; and director of operations and business development for Sightglass Coffee.

By 1995 Chuck Frank had decided he would rather be Larry's friend than his employee. Chuck joked that they canceled each other out on every corporate vote. After playing a key role in securing the Il Fornaio Burlingame location, he returned to his soon-again-thriving restaurant-consulting business. He and his wife Barbara and Faz Poursohi, the original MacArthur Park of Palo Alto chef, bought it when

Spectrum spun it off. Chuck sold it to Faz during the pandemic. He and Larry continue to enjoy a beautiful and legitimate fifty-year been-through-the-wars-together friendship.

Marsha Guerrero also departed in 1995. She wanted a life change. She was turning fifty in November and had promised herself a "big life adventure." Like Stanley, she signed on with Equinox Concepts and went to work in Singapore, where she stayed until 2000. When she returned she began working closely with legendary Chez Panisse founder Alice Waters, directing Waters' Edible Schoolyard Project.

Today Marsha credits working for Larry with preparing her to work with Alice. In her view, she could not have worked with uncompromising Alice if she hadn't worked for Larry first. She found the similarities between the two compelling.

A strong prioritization of beauty. A belief that everything should be aesthetically pleasing, but not an effort. An instinctive inclination to surround themselves with beautiful people and things. It's who they are and what they represent.

To Marsha's eye, both Alice and Larry are beautiful themselves: *just look at his hands, he's got beautiful hands!*

A self-described "aesthete" herself, Marsha realizes some people might consider such an orientation elitist or superficial. She doesn't.

"It's just *in* some people. They're artists. It doesn't have to be pretentious."

Reflecting on the phenomenal work ethic Larry and Alice share, Marsha observed, "It was hard. But it wasn't like going to work. The job changed every day. It was so rich. Larry really understood and taught me the pleasure of work. Family means so much to him, he's a wonderful father and grandfather. But in my experience, work came first for Larry."

Both Larry and Alice have a desire for recognition; they enjoy seeing their work and success acknowledged. Neither is coy nor falsely modest, says Marsha. Although each is quick to credit their associates and good fortune as well, both also understand themselves to be special in some way.

Marsha remembers her years at Spectrum and Il Fornaio with great warmth and gratitude.

"Larry pushed us. We pushed ourselves. We worked hard for the money. For most of the time, I was the only woman on the senior staff. I cried a lot. I never felt good enough. How many times, behind on a deadline, did I hear *Marsha! While we're young!?* But Larry mentored the hell out of us. If you were available, if you were paying attention, he wanted you to succeed. I wouldn't have bought a house if it weren't for Larry. I liked my apartment in the Haight. When he told me I needed to buy a house, I said I couldn't afford one. He said 'Bullshit. You make $40K a year. If you can shop at Wilkes Bashford, you can buy a house,' which I did; I never would have if he hadn't pushed me."

San Francisco Chronicle photographer John O'Hara, assigned to cover a Golden State Warriors game, couldn't resist this shot of Larry and son Nick; Oakland, California, 1994.

Here Comes Hislop

Shortly after Stanley, Chuck, and Marsha moved on, Mike Hislop arrived. Mike had previously been chairman and CEO of the Bay Area-based Chevy's Mexican Restaurants. He helped the company grow from seventeen to sixty-three locations nationwide under his direction. Building the company's infrastructure with an eye toward an initial public offering (IPO), he tried to make it as attractive to investors as possible. Chevy's fundamentals became so strong that the company never made it to the stock exchange. Instead, food and beverage giant PepsiCo, which included not only eponymous Pepsi-Cola but also Frito Lay, made a "crazy" offer to buy the company. Chevy's accepted.

Although Chevy's technically never went public, getting an arguably even better outcome, Hislop had put the company through the necessary paces to do so. As such, he had just the experience and expertise Larry was looking for.

Stanley may not have been interested in rapid growth and an IPO, but Larry was. Years before, Spectrum had grown organically. Larry, Jerry, and Chuck were flying by the seat of their pants. Again, there was no master plan, it was just *do the next thing, hope to hell the checks clear, and we'll see what happens after that*. But what Larry had seen of growth and finance during his time at Saga excited him.

Investment banker Warren Hellman and venture capitalist Scott Hedrick were on the Il Fornaio board, as was merchandiser Howard Lester, who had taken Williams Sonoma public in 1983. The expertise was there. Becoming a public company had been a goal for Il Fornaio from the start. It would be a long road to travel. The company first needed to prove it could grow privately, but eyes were definitely on that long-range prize.

There was also an emotional component for Larry: his father Sy had been president of Chock full o'Nuts, which was a publicly traded company. The idea that he, Larry, could not just run but *build* something equivalent to the company his dad had led motivated him greatly. Plus, as always with Larry, he unapologetically wanted to make money. Going public seemed a likely means to that desired end.

Hislop lived in Marin, and he knew Larry to some degree. Hislop had been in the Corte Madera, Levi's Plaza, and Del Mar restaurants. If Mike saw some inconsistencies, he also loved the brand and the passion behind it. Once the two men began to talk, things moved quickly. There was no headhunter involved. Il Fornaio soon had a new president and chief operating officer.

There had been one other candidate for the position. Readers would recognize the nationwide restaurant chains—veritable household names—he headed. Yet whereas everything about Mike Hislop felt right, solid and substantial, there was something about this other candidate that didn't feel quite right. Larry was even put off by his garish cuff links.

Ten years later, the flashy fellow pled guilty to fraud charges and was sentenced to thirteen months in prison for the misappropriation of funds. He had played fast and loose with the title to a Tuscan villa, among other irregularities.

Mike Hislop, fit and very secure, had a natural command presence, bringing to mind 49ers Hall of Famer Ronnie Lott: ferocious on the field, an absolute gentleman off it. Mike already respected and admired the company he was joining. With fresh, experienced eyes, he saw ways to build upon what already existed, further professionalizing management and systems. He knew the food was great and credited Larry for that.

"If someone made a cookie wrong, he'd lose his goddamn mind. He had an unbelievable palate. If a muffin or a brick chicken wasn't right, he'd go nuts. He was passionate about food, and food quality, passionate about chefs. He supported them, gave them whatever they wanted in the kitchen, state of the art. It was chef heaven. Italians wanted to work at Il Fornaio; it was the real deal. *Larry thought he was Italian.* He dragged me all over Italy, showing me—'this is where we got this, this is where we got that.' He was legit."

Mike's comment about Larry's palate is interesting. In more than one interview, Larry commented, "I know nothing about running a restaurant. I never cooked a dish or developed a wine list. I only worked the front in a pinch. I'm a serial entrepreneur. I negotiate deals, I trouble shoot, I battle landlords, I scout for sites. I'm grateful to my employees for being better at running restaurants than I am. I hire good people and pay them well."

Although a generous bit of self-effacement, Stanley Morris also asserted that Larry's sense of taste didn't get the credit it should. As he explained, "Larry's not a foodie, but he knows what he likes, and he has a great palate. It might go all the way back to those daily tasting sessions at Caswell."

It's unlikely Larry's companies would have performed as they have over the decades without a person who knew and loved food and restaurants at the top.

While Mike Hislop was tasked with preparing the company to go public, whether he knew it or not, he assumed another role as well. He became an invaluable mentor to Michael Mindel. Father and son worked well together—there was never any problem—but the younger man grew and flourished as an executive under Hislop. The dynamics of a father as boss or a son as protégé can be wonderful. All the same, in this case slipping the constraints of those roles was advantageous for each. For the company as well, since Hislop was such an outstanding coach.

In 1994 hotelier Richard Gunner, owner of the Pine Inn, Carmel's oldest and many say most picturesque and charming hotel, wanted Larry to open an Il Fornaio that would complement his establishment's tastefully quiet "personality." Larry was confident Il Fornaio could deliver. He was soon reminded that "each restaurant brings its own challenges."

The snag in Carmel was a city ordinance banning chain restaurants. The spirit of the rule made sense—no one wanted a McDonald's on Ocean Avenue, the quaint seaside village's main street. Carmel would be the tenth Il Fornaio; so, by letter-of-the-law definition, Larry's company was a chain. Following that logic, so was Tiffany & Co., the luxury jewelry, gifts, and accessories concern.

The reality was different: each Il Fornaio restaurant was its own entity. General managers and executive chefs were given great leeway to conceive and implement their own localized version of the company vision—hardly a standardized, cookie-cutter approach.

Larry believed he could convince the city council that the no-chain ordinance did not apply in Il Fornaio's case. He had loved the town ever since he moved to California decades before. He knew to his bones that the Carmel Il Fornaio would add to, rather than detract from, its character.

In an attempt to demonstrate good faith prior to the council meeting, Larry and Michael Mindel took "unchain-like" measures to meet the council partway. They even proposed a slightly different name for the proposed restaurant: Il Fornaio della Spiaggia (The Baker at the Beach). They also brought in a different designer to create a menu unlike those at existing Il Fornaios. The concept consisted of a completely different presentation, more rustic and Italian.

When Larry spoke to a combined audience of seventy-five council members and citizens, he encountered an unanticipated amount of pushback. "They put me through thirty minutes of agony, after we'd already put at least a hundred grand into initial design," he said. "Finally, I just lost it. I went off. I told them that all my adult life I have admired this town, dreamed of living here even someday. But tonight, after the way you have treated me and my request to give a town that can really use it a great Italian restaurant, I wouldn't live here if you had a gun to my head."

The genteel, Bach Festival-going crowd was taken aback, stunned into silence. Finally, a council member stood and said, "Mr. Mindel is 100 percent right, and we are wrong. We should approve his request and thank Il Fornaio for coming to town." His colleagues agreed and voted unanimously in favor of Il Fornaio.

One of Michael's friend's parents who lived in Carmel Valley attended the meeting. The friend's father, who could be prickly and stingy with praise, did not know Larry well. It wasn't common for him to praise another man. Michael's friend was therefore surprised and delighted when his father raved about Larry's performance, saying that it was his authenticity—"nothing phony about him at all"—that carried the vote.

If Carmel was an ongoing challenge for Larry, the legendary Italian actress Sophia Loren was a bright spot. The Amici Dell'Italia (Friends of Italy) Foundation put on "Una Serata con Sophia" ("An

Evening with Sophia") at the San Francisco Museum of Modern Art's new Third Street showplace. Italian style setters Giorgio Armani and Bulgari sponsored the event, as did Il Fornaio.

As stated earlier, while Larry values his many male friends, as he will readily admit, he *loves* women. Especially pretty ones like his wife Debby, his daughters Laura and Katherine, daughters-in-law Joni, Alicia, and Andrea, and granddaughters Eleanor, Louisa, and Collins. The *nebbish* from Toledo could not have been more thrilled to dine with the legendary actress Sophia Loren. As the invitation, which Il Fornaio produced in its familiar style and typeface, explained, "A unique and enduring beauty, a passionate performer, Sophia Loren embodies the warmth, earthiness, and sun-drenched nature of her native Italy."

Sophia and Larry were simpatico. "Loren's eroticism is that of the soul," said the *San Francisco Examiner* in an article previewing the event. Like Larry, for Sophia food was a matter of the heart, a sentiment she shared in that same article: "Food is something very passionate, very strong, very intense. It's more erotic than romantic. I like to cook for my friends. It is an act of love because in cooking you can create so many plates and recipes. I take pleasure in it because it's like a ceremony…"

Loren was enjoying a late-career renaissance. After winning her second Academy Award a couple years prior, this one for lifetime achievement, she was appearing in *Grumpier Old Men* and, three months before, had reprised her striptease from 1964's *Yesterday, Today and Tomorrow* in Robert Altman's *Ready to Wear*.

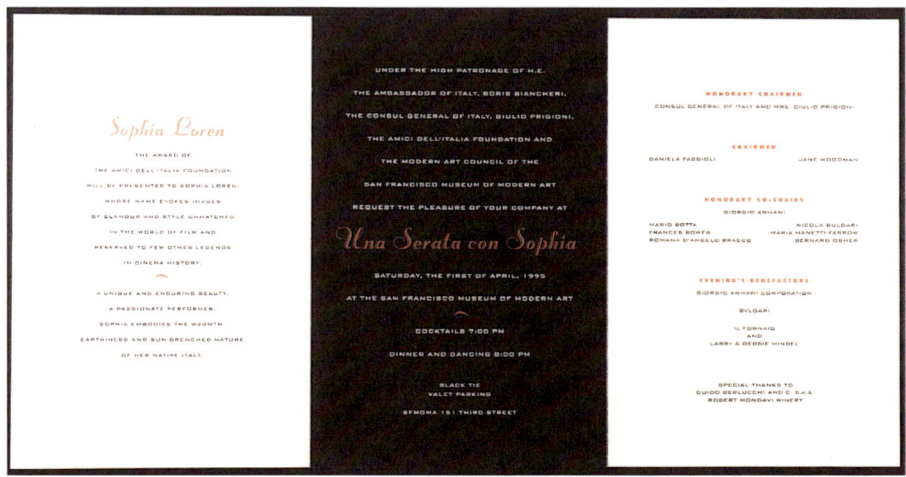

A *San Francisco Chronicle* interviewer asked her, "Has the cultural climate in Italy changed much since the days when the Vatican was criticizing your relationship with Carlo (her husband, whom she started seeing when she was fifteen and he was thirty-seven) and your friend Fellini for making immoral movies?"

Loren replied, "Giant steps have been done since then. Life goes on and life evolves. There are things that were bad then but now are more tolerated. And they do things today that we never *dreamed* of!"

Mike Hislop was also a bright spot for Larry. One of the things that drew Larry to Mike was the informal conversation they had before Larry extended the offer. During that interview, Larry was impressed by Mike's ability to candidly describe Il Fornaio as he experienced it. If Chevy's could be distilled down into two words—Fresh Mex, as in new salsa and tortillas prepared every hour—Mike felt Il Fornaio could be briefly encapsulated into "authentic Italian." He saw several important points of differentiation separating Il Fornaio from its competition: baking bread as it was traditionally baked in Italy; hiring first-generation Italian chefs almost exclusively; the company's annual chefs trip to Italy; house-label olive oil, coffee, and wine. All of it contributed to the authentic Italian experience customers valued.

In a sense, the new executive was just condensing into two words what Larry and others already knew. Eight years earlier, when the *Chronicle* had reviewed the very first Il Fornaio restaurant, in Corte Madera, Patty Unterman wrote, "Unlike other recently opened Italian spots in the Bay, Il Fornaio smacks of authenticity. It's there in the risotto, in the rotisserie chickens and rabbits, in the perfect crusted pizzas and focaccia…Il Fornaio is neither an imitation of Italian food nor a variation on Italian food. If there are mistakes, they are Italian mistakes. You can find the real thing in Corte Madera."

As Hislop settled in, he implemented several strategic initiatives to help the company grow and become more profitable—and therefore attractive to investors—with the ultimate goal of a public offering. He had executive chef Maurizio Mazzon compile a recipe book, which entailed reviewing the recipes, photographing the dishes, and writing out the details, including proper pronunciation, then distributing them to chefs throughout the company. More complex endeavors included figuring out which points of differentiation truly were central to the company's success, which made economic sense and which did not.

One inefficiency that Mike convinced Larry to confront was the labor-intensive nature of the small bakeries attached to each restaurant. It took a lot of people working long hours to bake all that bread and all those savories, just as it did to make every sauce and dessert in the restaurants from scratch. Something had to give.

It was hard for anyone affiliated with the company from the start to imagine an Il Fornaio restaurant that *didn't* have a bakery on site. The bakeries felt like the heart of each restaurant, and they contributed to an overall sense of authenticity. There were thousands of these stand-alone bakeries in Italy. Attaching a restaurant to the bakery was Larry's brilliant add-on. They were hugely successful—but add-ons nonetheless.

Newcomer Mike saw this more objectively than Larry could. He suggested they build a large wholesale bakery to service all the restaurants in northern California. The bakery could also supply the same fresh, award-winning breads and pastries to quality grocery stores, specialty retailers, and other fine-dining restaurants. The single, large new bakery would provide efficiencies in production—both with regards to labor and ingredients—and distribution, as well as the capacity to grow Il Fornaio's business. Product quality could not suffer, however; it would be counterproductive if it did, no matter how impressive the financial gains.

The company pulled it off, opening a 12,000 square foot wholesale bakery in Burlingame in March 1997. Surprisingly, quality actually improved.

According to a marketing blurb: "The bakery produces over 30 varieties of bread and rolls based on regional Italian recipes, as well as a wide assortment of Italian cookies, cakes and pastries. Recipes are standardized to ensure consistency. Our bread doughs, based on centuries-old recipes, are mixed and then fermented for up to 20 hours to increase flavor. Each loaf is hand-formed, proofed and baked in European deck ovens that eject steam around the bread at timed intervals. These processes contribute to a characteristically irregular-shaped and crusty bread…Some recipes include fresh aromatic herbs and spices, such as rosemary or fennel, or other ingredients, such as Parmesan cheese, raisins, nuts and sesame seeds."

A vision came into clear focus, utilizing "the power of three." Il Fornaio believed that its trinity—restaurants, wholesale bakeries, and retail markets—would work together to secure the company's place as the top provider of premium quality, authentic Italian food.

Small retail markets incorporated into the design of each restaurant contributed to the trattorias' distinctive, authentic Italian atmosphere. They offered Il Fornaio-brand items, including fresh baked goods, oakwood-roasted coffee, pasta, risotto, extra virgin olive oil, and balsamic vinegar imported from Modena. Guests could also buy an Il Fornaio-brand Chianti Classico from a Tuscan vineyard originally planted in the eleventh century. The vineyard was designated for Il Fornaio's exclusive use.

As Larry wrote in the company's 1997 annual report, "A new niche is evolving in the restaurant business, somewhere between 'casual dining' with an average guest check of $15 and 'fine dining' where a guest routinely pays in excess of $50. We call this new niche 'sophisticated dining.' Our definition of sophisticated dining applies to the handful of restaurant groups that offer great food, professional service, beautiful and worldly-wise environments, but with a check average of *under* $25. Two separate company-sponsored research studies indicate that our customers dine at Il Fornaio an average of sixteen times per year, a visitation normally associated with quick-service restaurants."

This was in line with Larry's "affordable luxury" mantra, and it fit perfectly with Hislop's intent to "drive frequency." Mike was always eager to welcome new guests, but his main objective was to find ways to entice established customers to come in more often. Sixteen visits per year was nice, but why not twenty-five—once every two weeks—or better yet, fifty, which equated to once a week? Building new restaurants was a fun and exciting way to grow, but it also entailed some risk. It was much safer to court an existing customer base.

Like Larry, Mike Hislop and Michael Mindel both believed that "providing an authentic Italian dining experience by offering quality food and bakery products, distinctive décor, five-star service and an attractive price-value relationship is the most effective approach to attracting new and repeat guests." But "the Mikes" also believed there were specific things they could do to increase repeat visits.

They created the *Festa Regionale* loyalty promotion program, with innovative monthly menus developed by chef-partners, based on authentic recipes from one of Italy's twenty geographic regions. Mailers describing each month's *Festa Regionale* offerings were sent to more than 100,000 households identified through customer mailing lists or geographic proximity to an Il Fornaio. Members who participated in the program received a "passport stamp" from that region if they ordered one of the special menu items. Similar to the S&H Green Stamps of yesteryear, those who filled their *passaporto* by collecting at least one stamp a month for six consecutive months earned a commemorative plate, as well as entry in a raffle for an all-expenses-paid trip to Italy. Laura Mindel was an avid, if perhaps not perfectly eligible participant, given her father and brother's roles in the company—but she really wanted that plate.

Public and Private

Il Fornaio Portland opened in 1996, an important development, since to go public the company needed to prove it could grow beyond California. P.J. Carlesimo, coach of National Basketball Association team the Trail Blazers, was a regular customer, often hosting postgame dinners at the restaurant.

The next big move was Las Vegas, where New York-New York Hotel opened in January 1997. *The Las Vegas Sun* described it as "quite a wonderful place, with such whimsical re-creations of its namesake city as a lifelike, scaled-down version of the skyline, Lady Liberty in New York Harbor (complete with a small tugboat), a walking-sized Brooklyn Bridge and storefront exteriors. Inside, on the walkway into Little Italy, manholes emit steam and postal boxes are covered with graffiti. Boxy room air conditioners protrude from the windows of apartments, located just like the real thing, above the stores. Stroll through a Central Park highlighted with tall, spreading, lifelike trees and banks of slot machines…"

Following a trend that was beginning to emerge for large resorts, New York-New York did not plan to run any of its several restaurants itself, turning instead to restaurateurs like Larry with proven track records.

Initially Larry didn't jump at New York-New York's offer. He worried that opening in the hotel, which, like almost every other hotel in Las Vegas would include a casino, might besmirch Il Fornaio's reputation. Il Fornaio's board of directors shared or maybe even prompted Larry's concern.

"You should have seen the looks on the board members' faces when Larry told them he might open in Vegas. What a long shot then. That took friggin' balls. He deserves full credit on that one," Mike Hislop recalled.

It wasn't an overnight decision for Larry. He fretted over it: would Il Fornaio's image fit with Las Vegas? He asked Sin City's largest builder of hotels what he thought.

"Are you kidding me?" the man replied. "Do you want to make money? Don't be a fool. Open here and you will succeed."

That nudged Larry closer. He walked out of the meeting thinking he'd do it. But when negotiations with the hotel dragged on, Larry's resolve faltered.

After New York-New York's frustrated owners flew to San Francisco to convince Larry to agree, everyone—including Larry—thought the deal was on. But he had one final bout of uncertainty, hesitating when it came time to sign actual papers. Exasperated, his counterpart on the other side shouted, "Do you want to make fucking money? Then sign the fucking papers!"

Larry did, to his everlasting relief and gratitude.

"I was so lucky. I almost blew that opportunity. It's good to be lucky."

The restaurant got off to a scorching start, hotter than any Il Fornaio ever. It has stayed strong ever since, doing eight figures annually, an exceptional performance for a restaurant.

Larry attributes much of the success to managing partner Lino Chini, who opened Del Mar so successfully, describing him in the *Sun* as "the consummate restaurateur, from his passion for great Italian food to his dedication to warm professional service. Lino operates at a level seldom seen in this business."

Il Fornaio at New York-New York turned out to be more than just a top performer for the company. If Larry had elected not to open there, he would have passed on not only a reliable gold mine that has enriched Il Fornaio's coffers for more than twenty-five years, but also a key to the company's public offering later in 1997—something he and other people in the know, like Mike Hislop and Michael Mindel, readily acknowledge. If New York-New York hadn't burst from the gate as powerfully as it did those first few months, "a grand slam," in Mike Hislop's words, confirming exponentially what Portland had begun to prove—that the company could prosper beyond the Golden State—investors might not have supported the IPO.

Despite those and other successes, Larry wasn't always right.

Starbucks founder Howard Schultz came to Larry in the early 1990s, proposing a Starbucks-Il Fornaio ("our coffee, your pastries") joint venture. Although Larry liked and admired Howard, he passed on the offer.

"My company was bigger than his company," Larry later laughed, reflecting on the missed opportunity. "Why would I want to partner with him?"

The black-tie New York-New York opening night party wasn't just another work night; it was a personal watershed as well, the first of Larry's ("Nonno's") career to include not only children but also grandchildren. Guests of honor included Michael's son Dashiel and Laura's son Sam, who was born the year before. That night Joni Mindel, Michael's wife, shattered frumpy baby-mom stereotypes by out-glamming and out-dancing her new best friend, Vanna White, *Wheel of Fortune* game show co-host.

Vegas was the final piece of the going-public puzzle. When a company goes public, some of its shares become available for purchase on a stock exchange; the Nasdaq, in Il Fornaio's case. The company works with an investment bank to write up a prospectus, basically an "open book" for those who might want to purchase shares. The prospectus tells the company story in detail: who the owners and senior managers are; how much they make; what they have accomplished; what their vision or plan is for the future; what risks an investor might assume if they choose to buy the stock. The company submits the prospectus to the Securities Exchange Commission (SEC), which sends it back with revisions. The company and investment bank make the changes and resubmit, sometimes repeatedly.

Once the lead underwriter (investment bank) gets SEC approval on the prospectus, several investment bankers and a handful of the company's top executives embark on a roadshow, meeting with institutions and brokers around the country to introduce the forthcoming stock. While the travel can be grueling, questions and comments from prospective buyers can be even more so: *Why should we buy this stock or encourage our customers to? Do you really know what you're doing? Maybe you've just gotten lucky so far.*

Venture-backed companies like Il Fornaio are not intended to stay private. By definition, some portion—sometimes a large one—of the company's original start-up money comes from firms or individuals with an expectation that, in a not-too-distant future, the company will find itself in one of two scenarios: it will be successful enough to be bought by another company, or it will go public. Either way, early investors are rewarded for their smart bet.

Venture capitalists often put together and promote funds that have a defined life, typically five or ten years. Investors invest their money with the expectation that at the end of that period they will get it back, ideally with a significant return, in accordance with how well companies in the fund perform.

Money invested in a private company is not typically available on demand. It is illiquid, tied up in the company. In order for a fund to get back the money it originally invested, the investment needs to transform from illiquid to liquid, or readily available. Most commonly that happens when a company is either sold or goes public, both being "liquidity events." Money that was tied up becomes available.

According to *Forbes* magazine, when Larry bought the eight original money-losing bakeries from Williams Sonoma in 1986, he raised $2.5 million in venture capital and invested $200,000 of his own. From the start, Il Fornaio intended eventually either to get bought or go public, converting the illiquid investment into liquid cash. There was no guarantee it would happen. The company, under Larry's direction, would have to perform, a bracing competitive and potentially remunerative challenge.

Following an IPO, companies usually benefit from increased brand visibility and credibility. Public companies are often perceived as a bigger deal, more legitimate than private companies, whether or not that's true. They typically receive more attention from the press, making it easier for other companies to know about and evaluate them for potential acquisition. Recruiting and retaining talented employees and executives is often easier for a public company than for a private one, especially when the company offers stock options and equity-based compensation, as Il Fornaio did for general managers and executive chefs. Employees' financial interests become directly tied to the company's performance and growth, promoting a sense of ownership and dedication. They have skin in the game.

There were good reasons for Il Fornaio to go public, but no factor figured more prominently in the decision than Larry's dogged determination, what he called emotion-backed resolve.

"A lot of that emotion—most of that emotion—was my dad, the only hero I have ever had. He ran a public company. Once I realized that I had the experience, skill, and opportunity to not just manage a public company as he did but to actually build a small private business into something that was big enough and good enough to take public, I had to do it. I wasn't competing against my dad or trying to surpass him, not at all. I was standing upon his shoulders, building off a foundation he had laid. He wasn't with me anymore, but we were doing it together. Many times during the run-up to the IPO I would look up and say, 'Can you believe this, Dad?'"

Las Vegas opened at the beginning of January 1997. Larry's dad died at the end of the month. By summer Larry and Mike Hislop were on the Il Fornaio roadshow, which began in San Francisco.

A finance man raised his hand after their first presentation and asked, "Larry, why on earth would I want to put money into a restaurant company? Your story doesn't grab me, doesn't impress me."

Larry was crestfallen.

"What have I gotten myself into?" he asked himself. "How could I be so dumb?"

When that same man signed for the maximum number of shares he could secure, Larry's doubts were assuaged.

Despite that initial hiccup, the hectic, high-adrenaline national roadshow turned out to be a blast. Meeting smart new people every day and talking up a company in which he believed so strongly came naturally to Larry. The wins mounted.

Off hours, he and Hislop, restaurant lifers, talked brand and evolution of brand deep into the night. The locked-in ex-athletes didn't allow themselves the reward of a celebratory evening martini until close to trip's end, when it was clear all shares offered would be purchased.

After the strong roadshow, Il Fornaio and underwriters Montgomery Securities and Alex Brown elected to price the stock slightly higher than originally planned. As the *San Francisco Chronicle* explained on Sept 20, 1997, following the company's robust debut: "Acting more like a technology stock than a restaurant stock, shares of Il Fornaio closed up 32 percent on the company's first day of public trading. Shares of the San Francisco-based chain of upscale Italian eateries closed at $14.50 yesterday on the Nasdaq. The initial offering price of $11 was already higher than the $9 to $10.50 planned in August when the company announced intent to go public."

Larry was elated. He and the team had done it.

In simple terms, they only had "given up" roughly 20 percent of the company. In return, they received $11 million, money they quickly put to good use. In November they opened in Santa Monica. In December they opened in Denver, three blocks from Coors Field. The following year, 1998, they opened in Seattle and Walnut Creek.

In 1999 Il Fornaio opened in Atlanta, Coronado, Manhattan Beach, and Scottsdale, before doubling down on Vegas, where they opened Canaletto at the Venetian Resort, just two miles from New York-New York. After developer Sheldon Adelson razed the venerable Sands Hotel and Casino, which had occupied the site since 1952, and began to build the more than 4,000 room-Venetian, he asked Larry if he wanted to open a restaurant there.

Larry was intrigued. New York-New York was flourishing, so he knew Il Fornaio could win in Vegas, especially in a resort on the scale of Adelson's. There was also a smaller but still enticing emotional component: Mimi's dad, Sonny, had been a regular at—perhaps even an investor in—the Sands, which was known for its elegant italic "Sands" neon sign with a giant uppercase S and its world-renowned Copa Room nightclub. It had been home to Frank Sinatra, Dean Martin, Jerry Lewis, and Sammy Davis Jr., as well as other noteworthy entertainers. The stunning Copa Girls–"the most beautiful girls in the world"–had also called it home.

Larry felt recently departed Sonny—the onetime Spectrum and Caswell board member whom he loved and respected like a father—tapping him on the shoulder, encouraging him to give the deal close consideration.

After mulling over the opportunity, Larry decided to open a restaurant that was *not* an Il Fornaio. This was a departure. Following Etrusca's closure after three short years, the company had elected to laser in on just one concept, Il Fornaio—and Il Fornaio only—in preparation for the public offering.

But there was already an Il Fornaio at New York-New York, two short miles away. It was too close, too successful, too well-known. Larry set out to do something deliberately different. Given the grand scope and nature of Adelson's dream, Larry saw it as a chance to create an Il Fornaio that was even better than Il Fornaio—fancier and more expensive, harkening back to Etrusca, a ristorante rather than a trattoria.

He and native Veneto Executive Chef Maurizio Mazzon dreamed up and delivered Canaletto Ristorante Veneto, "the ultimate Venetian dining experience." Adelson's resort was over the top, like a New York-New York on steroids, with replicas of Venice landmarks, including the Doge's Palace, the Rialto Bridge, and a 315-foot-high replica of St. Mark's Campanile. Canaletto sat in the middle of St. Mark's Square, overlooking the gondola-filled Grand Canal.

Larry negotiated with the president of Adelson's company, as well as its director of real estate, securing what he considered "a hell of a lease." Adelson himself was not thrilled when he learned the terms. He once said, "I'm the son of a Boston cab driver, and no one ever gave me anything for nothing."

The deal turned out well for both parties, despite the fact that—if Michael Mindel is to be believed—Adelson "loathed" the lease until the end of his days.

When he died in 2021, *Forbes* estimated Adelson's net worth at just under $30 billion. He had donated more money than anyone else to Donald Trump's 2016 presidential campaign.

The resort and restaurant opened May 3, 1999, providing Larry an opportunity to catch up with his SF MOMA inamorata, VIP guest Sophia Loren.

Like Loren, Canaletto has proved to be timeless. Thanks in part to the 2023 addition of the on-property entertainment venue Sphere, today it's going stronger than ever. Michael Mindel enjoyed both on his sixtieth birthday, celebrating with dinner at Canaletto, followed by a concert at Sphere.

Larry more than met the challenge of leading a publicly traded company. As the months grew into years, however, he also gained perspective that only someone who has led both private and public companies can appreciate. He began to experience firsthand the unique constraints and pressures public companies face, such as the need for constant growth, regardless of whether it's right for the company.

"Growing restaurants rapidly really isn't my thing. I try to do one restaurant at a time and make that the best restaurant I know how. If over time that turns out to be successful, I'll do another. But usually after we open, I swear I will never open another restaurant, ever. Fortunately, that feeling always passes."

The pressure not only to grow constantly, opening ever more restaurants, but also to make more money each quarter ate at Larry. No one wanted more intensely for the company to prosper than he did. And it wasn't as though he'd ever operated solo before Il Fornaio went public. He'd always been accountable to boards of directors and investors.

Now, though, he found himself in new circumstances, ones that quickly grew tiresome. He didn't like dealing with outside financial analysts who passed judgement on the company's performance over short blocks of time, without full knowledge of its longer-range plans or current extenuating circumstances.

The company hired a real estate specialist in response to the growth imperative, in essence an attempt to clone Larry. Site selection and lease negotiation had always been his domain. The idea was for them to continue to be his domain, but for someone else to do it as well. The company could investigate and secure at least twice as many locations if it doubled the manpower devoted to the task.

It didn't take long for Larry to realize he didn't like the new set-up. He had no personal quibble with the new man, but for Larry the site-selection role had always been and ideally always would be his and his alone.

He rued the company's relatively short-lived Scottsdale, Arizona location.

"It was below grade. Below grade!"

The other fellow found and recommended the site, and harried Larry ultimately approved it. Upon reflection years later he was certain: had he himself, working at a sustainable pace, been the sole selector, Il Fornaio would not have opened in that spot.

Regulatory compliance was no joy either. Public companies must adhere to strict reporting standards. All his career—at Caswell, Spectrum, Saga, and Il Fornaio—Larry lived by the numbers, as he still does today, staying current on his restaurants' nightly and annual sales and expenses.

He never tried to deceive or mislead investors or board members when he led private companies. Everyone always had all the pertinent information. But public reporting, with its comprehensive financial audits, legal consultations, filing and listing fees, and governance and transparency expenses, was an entirely different and more expensive animal, in 2000 costing $400,000. It was a pain in the neck and felt like overkill.

As the new millennium dawned, Larry began to realize that leading a public company might not be all he had imagined it to be. He had no regrets about taking Il Fornaio public: he remained convinced it was the right thing to do at the time, for business as well as for personal reasons. Now, though, he was one of the relatively few leaders who could make an informed comparison, who knew both the costs and benefits of public as well as private ownership.

Shares of Il Fornaio stock traded as low as $4.50 and as high as $17 in the first three years it was public. Restaurant analyst Michael Smith of Fahnestock & Co noted that "extremely wide earnings swings" and "missed profit estimates" undermined investor confidence in Il Fornaio. It wasn't a *bad* stock, but it was somewhat ordinary in comparison to the hot new technology ones taking off at the time.

Larry and the board had options. They could continue on, running the business to the best of their ability, living with the publicly-traded-company headaches. They could also consider a sale. Outback Steakhouse, Inc. of Tampa made extended overtures, but a deal fell through when the two companies could not agree on a price.

In November 2000, Il Fornaio decided to "go private." They would sell the company to East Coast private equity firm Bruckmann, Rosser, Sherrill & Co. (BRS). BRS would own and grow Il Fornaio at a manageable pace, before selling or taking it public again, as they had done with California Pizza Kitchen. BRS wanted everyone who worked at the company to stay. No shake-ups were planned.

BRS was the perfect buyer. They had a solid track record: consumer-product wins with AMF Bowling, Remington Arms, and Isotoner gloves. More importantly, in addition to California Pizza Kitchen, they had restaurant investment experience with companies such as Au Bon Pain and McCormick & Schmick's. They understood successful restaurant operation, and they immediately recognized that Larry and his associates were an exceptional team. Not only would micromanagement be unnecessary, it would be counterproductive.

Privatization was wonderful for Larry. He could finally monetize his shares in Il Fornaio. More entrepreneur than financier at heart, finance was not his native tongue—his speech nonetheless could be peppered with financial terms when called for by the topic at hand. He couldn't sell much stock in Il Fornaio when the company went public in 1997, nor did he want to. He was "locked up," required to hold on to his shares for six months following the offering.

In the period that followed, investor confidence and his own strong belief in the company dictated he remain a significant shareholder. People would be more likely to buy shares in Il Fornaio if they knew the top man was still heavily invested, and Larry loved betting on himself and his team: "Why wouldn't I want to have stock that I *knew* would only become more valuable over time?"

He was pleased when the opportunity to cash out presented itself. He sold roughly half of his stock. At sixty-three, Larry saw the opportunity as good for both the company and for him and his family. Shareholders agreed: they voted to delist from the Nasdaq and sell to Bruckmann.

By this time, Larry explained, "Mike Hislop was running the company. I was doing deals—that was important—but Mike was basically running the company."

Significant shareholder—and now chairman of the board rather than CEO—Larry still worked as hard as ever, retaining his office at Il Fornaio headquarters in Corte Madera. But the sale was a huge relief.

Although Il Fornaio announced its decision to go private in late 2000, the specific terms of the deal—$14 per share, about $81 million total—were neither finalized nor did the transaction close until July 2001.

Buona fortuna, or good luck, is rarely far from Larry's mind. He knows he has made sacrifices and worked very hard, but he's also aware that quite a few things have broken his way.

The World Trade Center and Pentagon attacks happened mere weeks after close of sale. The economy tanked. Michael Mindel would later point out there was no way Il Fornaio would have gotten the price they did if they had closed after—rather than immediately prior to—the heinous attacks.

As for the attacks themselves, as soon as Larry learned of the atrocity, he rushed to Branson, the Marin high school all of his children attended. He served two different terms as president of the board of trustees at Branson, which currently was conducting a search for a new headmaster. As board chair, Larry was one of the three people leading the school during this interregnum; acting head Jani Ross and chief financial officer Wayne Taylor were the other two.

When he got to the school, Larry conferred with Jani and Wayne. No one knew what might happen next—more attacks could be imminent. Jani, Wayne, and Larry all felt a heavy sense of responsibility for the 320 young lives—Larry and Debby's son, sophomore Nick, among them—and sixty faculty and staff entrusted to their care.

Larry spoke briefly to the entire school community, offering the leadership and reassurance everyone craved at that uncertain time.

Although Hislop continued to assume more and more responsibility at Il Fornaio, some days Larry still faced formidable challenges.

Few were more daunting than having to ask a founding board member to resign.

The Securities and Exchange Commission had detected some irregularities and notified Il Fornaio they were investigating. They suspected that the board member had used a relative's name to buy a significant amount of Il Fornaio stock prior to the sale announcement. He then profited nicely when the stock rose substantially with the news. Assuming it was true, it constituted illegal insider trading.

No charges were filed, but even the appearance of impropriety was problematic. Il Fornaio's attorney advised Larry he should ask the man to resign from the board and to insist that any profits realized be returned. Larry's "stomach was in (his) shoes" when he went to the man's office. It was an extremely difficult conversation. They were friends—he was fond of the fellow. The man was curt. He resigned, and, to Larry's dismay, they never talked again.

If some days were tough, Sunday evenings were anything but; instead, they were consistently fulfilling for Larry and his family.

Larry hosted an open early dinner at the original Il Fornaio in Corte Madera. Any available children or grandchildren who wanted to attend were welcome. Before Larry's youngest two children went off to college, a typical table might include Michael and Joni Mindel and their sons, Dash and Al; Laura and Steve, along with their sons, Sam and Henrik; Katherine and Nick; Debby and Larry. Tony and Mimi often came from the city as well. Later iterations included Tony's wife, Alicia, and their sons, Oscar and Renzo.

Larry's unique constellation of talents, indefatigable work ethic, and deep generosity combined to deliver many wonderful experiences for his family. Although some of those experiences were arguably more "glamorous" than the Sunday night dinners—Italy, Montana, Aspen, Hawaii, courtside Warrior seats—family members expressed special gratitude for those meals.

They liked the great food, being able to order as much of whatever they wanted, and the lightning-quick service—the large group was often in and out in an hour. Many of the servers were long tenured. Since Il Fornaio was a good place to work, they stayed put. The sprawling Mindel family and staff got to know and like each another.

One server in particular, Sherri, was an absolute godsend for Laura and her husband. The oldest daughter of a large upstate New York farm family, Sherri was familiar with babies. She'd been comforting them all her life. Laura would often arrive for dinner drained—as a new parent can be—place her order, and be able to eat her dinner in precious peace: Sherri would calmly and magically disappear with baby Sam while she ate. Did someone else cover her tables? Did she lug Sam about as she served other diners? A mystery to this day, but an incredible gift at that challenging time.

Dinners with Larry, the *capo dei capi* ("boss of bosses"), made some of his guests feel special. They enjoyed eating with him, basking in the reflected glory at the owner's table, which included not only outstanding food and service, but often a little ego boost as well. Larry paid using the *Persona Molto Importante* (PMI) card Il Fornaio issued to executives and investors. His account number was 001; Debby's was 002.

Larry's grandsons had their own take on the dinners. Henrik felt "big league" to get to make his own pizza. A waiter would bring him a rolled-out crust, along with small dishes of tomato sauce, pepperoni, cheese, and basil. Returning shortly after, they would whisk whatever pie Henrik had created off to the pizza oven. He felt special, something everyone should get to feel occasionally, in right measure.

Al might have felt a little *too* singled out one night. He and his brother and cousins peeled away from the table to go off on their own, as was customary once they finished their food. The Town Center mall felt like a familiar playground to the boys, who were there so often.

Al assumed the restaurant's pay phone would work only if he inserted a quarter. He deposited no money and "pretend dialed" several numbers, including 911. To his surprise and mortification, Corte Madera's finest rolled up minutes later.

More than one grandchild wrote a "Sunday Night Dinner" high school or college admission essay, using phrases like "mainstay of my childhood," "Nonno kept it friendly, but I definitely received the message," "many different points of view," and "laughter and joy."

Poggio

Some people—maybe even Larry himself—believed or hoped he would now shift into "fishing mode," that this transition time would mark the beginning of a hard-earned traditional retirement. He would no longer have to fly somewhere forty-eight weeks out of every fifty-two. He could spend more time in Montana, in Italy, on his boat, and with his grandchildren.

Life was good. Larry remained relevant. Il Fornaio executives and staff, from Hislop on down, still sought his advice. People outside the company came knocking, too, wanting his ideas on this location or that concept, as they always had.

Larry agreed to a meeting when representatives of Sausalito's newly expanded Casa Madrona Hotel asked to pick his brain. Of course he would advise as he could. Sausalito was his hometown.

John Mays had owned the historic hotel for many years. Wanting to expand in the late 1990s, he bought the adjacent Village Fair. Once a parking garage for Sausalito ferry passengers, it had been transformed into a unique shopping arcade, filled with small boutiques selling unusual, often imported merchandise not found anywhere else. By the time Mays bought the deteriorating building, the Village Fair marketing concept—copied in many other places, such as San Francisco's Ghirardelli Square and The Cannery—had run its course.

The old building required extensive seismic upgrades. Mays decided to sell a majority interest in the hotel to Dallas-based Olympus Real Estate Group. Olympus completed a thirty-one room and suite expansion and added a "world-class" health spa by June 2002. They asked to meet with Larry.

Their next move was to have a great restaurant in the hotel, one that would be more of a special amenity than a source of profit, a place that would differentiate the hotel from others in the area and help attract more guests.

The hotel's restaurant was on the fourth floor. Larry told them he was a firm believer in street-level restaurants. The Olympus people countered that there wasn't much room on the ground floor.

"So what?" Larry scoffed. "You really want to do this? Find a way to get more room on the ground floor."

He wasn't being flip or cavalier. They asked for his experienced, successful opinion, and he gave it to them. It wasn't his project. He wasn't overly attached.

"What about bathrooms?" they wondered.

"What about them?" Larry answered. "Put them on the second floor if you need to. But if you want a really great restaurant, you need to put it at street level."

He enjoyed speaking as an unpaid outside consultant. The company had solicited his expert advice at the city council's suggestion. Larry loved Sausalito, and he was happy to help those who wanted to make the town even better.

Not long after that meeting, Olympus thanked Larry for his ideas, then asked him to operate the dream restaurant he had described to them.

"No thanks," he laughed. "I'm supposed to be retired!"

Their offer was flattering, and it did strike a chord, however faintly. It made him realize that, although he appreciated his current relative freedom, he also missed the thrills that came with his previous responsibilities. "I'm a junkie. There's no better high than a full restaurant," he has said more than once.

When Olympus persisted, Larry half-jokingly said, "Okay, here would be my terms if I were to do it. I'm not saying I *will* do it, but—if I do—I would need to pay no minimum monthly rent, just a percentage of sales. I would not pay common area maintenance. And we would need free valet parking for our customers."

Michael Mindel, playing off Larry's grandkids' nickname for him, as well as the three negatives central to his terms—no minimum rent, no CAM, and no valet charge—called it the "Nonno Deal."

Larry was far from certain the owners would agree to those terms. A truly reluctant restaurateur at this point in his life, he had proven everything he needed to prove, in business and in life—to himself, his father, the world. He had nothing to lose by being as honest as he could in the ongoing conversations. He didn't consider it a negotiating ploy to say, "I am not looking to start a new restaurant. I am happy with my wonderful life as it is, but if I *were* to open a new place, here's what it would take." It was simply his truth.

When Olympus surprised him by agreeing to all three provisions, he realized just how content he was with life as it was. He was flattered—*they must* really *want me*—but his internal response to their agreement showed that he still didn't want to open the restaurant. It was something he couldn't know in advance, something that only became clear in the unfolding.

He and his family—Debby in particular—had earned his active rest. Again, he wasn't negotiating, consciously trying to squeeze the best deal he could out of a counterpart. He still saw himself as a hometown helper or consultant. Olympus's requests were part of the larger conversation to his mind. He was trying to help them realize they wanted someone *like* him, not him. He was unavailable.

They came back once more. This time they asked, "Larry, what would it take for you to open a restaurant in our hotel? We really want this to happen. Tell us what we need to do."

This got his attention in a way that nothing else had to that point. Realizing they were truly serious and that there might be a remarkable opportunity before him, he asked himself: *What* would *it take? What* do *I want? What's important to me?*

If he went back into the game, he wanted to retain some semblance of the newfound simplicity and sanity in his life; fewer headaches in the years to come, rather than more. One way to achieve that would be to get a piece of the hotel, to become a partner rather than just a tenant. Most landlords talked a good *we're on the same team, a rising tide lifts all boats* game, but in Larry's experience, at some point landlord-tenant relations almost always became adversarial. It was just the nature of the setup. Becoming a partial owner of the hotel might eliminate potential conflict down the line, the sorts of headaches he wanted to avoid. Restaurateur and hotelier really would be on the same team.

After Olympus surprised him yet again by agreeing not only to the Nonno Deal but also to the equity share, Larry elected to rejoin the restaurant game.

He acted quickly, telling his lawyer, close friend, and Montana compadre Tom Hyde about this latest development. Tom, Il Fornaio's longtime general counsel, helpfully talked Larry through the legal requirements and business challenges a new restaurant was most likely face: *Have you thought about this? Be ready for that.*

The Il Fornaio to BRS sale made Larry "more money than I had ever dreamed of." He could have poured much of that windfall right back into this new restaurant. He also could have financed it through a combination of his own money and a bank loan.

As he and Tom talked, he decided he would rather they both invite friends and businesspeople they knew to form a limited partnership. This would both spread the financial risk—Larry's wouldn't be the only neck on the block—and create an instant source of influential word-of-mouth support for the fledgling enterprise, the new restaurant in Sausalito.

Tom had served as counsel to venture capital firms. Raising money was not unfamiliar territory for him. Several times before, Larry's Chicago restaurant buddy and head of Lettuce Entertain You, Rich Melman, had done exactly what Larry and Tom wanted to do. He generously shared his experience.

They decided upon a private placement of $2 million dollars (build-out and operating capital)—forty partner shares at $50,000 each. They sent out a letter to pre-selected individuals whom Larry wanted to have as backers, folks he knew to be reasonable and low on the potential headache scale. Restaurants—even Larry Mindel restaurants—are never surefire investments. Partners had to understand that going in, as well as be able to gracefully absorb the hit if the new place didn't take off.

Positive responses came back quickly: people wanted in. That was encouraging.

Larry's next step was to meet with a designer, Anthony Fish of Arcanum Architecture. Larry still believed, as he always had, that beautiful, sophisticated design was vital to his restaurants' success, both at Spectrum and at Il Fornaio.

With each day, the new restaurant became a more personal passion project for Larry. No longer the head of a company employing more than a thousand people, he could throw himself into every last detail of his nascent creation.

He cherished his run with Howard Backen—the Sausalito house, the Montana lodge, and the first seventeen Il Fornaios—but in age and stature Howard was like a brother. Fish, just a year older than Michael Mindel, likely felt closer to a son. That included being more "malleable," Larry joked without disparagement. It was simply an acknowledgement that on this project, he not only could but wanted to be more involved on the design side than he'd ever been before.

Fish proved to be an excellent collaborator. With clarity and skill not every designer would have demonstrated, he successfully heard, saw, and made tangible Larry's vision.

Part of Larry's design research included a trip to Italy with now-partner Tom Hyde. Again, nice work if you can get it!

Larry created photo albums containing pictures from many of the thirty Italy trips he took over the course of his career. The albums included details like odd little closeups of doors, floors, or plates. When he saw something he liked, he took a picture or jotted down a note, things he could incorporate into a restaurant upon return home.

The travel was fun, but it was work, too—work on behalf of thousands of diners. Some had never been and would never get to Italy. Thanks to Larry's efforts, they would be able to enjoy its very best without ever leaving the United States.

Tom enjoys looking around the restaurant today and seeing the fruits of that scouting trip: the beautiful wall sconces; the floor nearly identical to the one in a high-end hotel in Florence; the entry door and bar from another hotel across the Arno.

"Larry has an amazing eye for detail," Tom observed, as so many others have through the years.

The restaurant's initial working name was Cantinetta. Larry liked the sound of it, and he believed that it fit with his vision for the trattoria.

At Thanksgiving in 2002, he was seated next to a young Italian exchange student staying with friends of Mimi. Larry outlined his plans to her, including the restaurant's location at the bottom of the hill and the name Cantinetta.

She smiled, eyes sparkling, and exclaimed, "No, you should call it Il Poggio instead! It means something like 'a special place on a hill.'"

Enchanted by her pronunciation of the word and fueled by holiday cheer, Larry dropped the "Il" and played with "Poggio," saying it to himself several times.

It's one thing to espouse an "if you're open to it" philosophy. It's another to act on it repeatedly, as Larry has over the years. He decided that night that the restaurant would be named Poggio. In hindsight it's hard to imagine the restaurant as anything else. The name looks, sounds, and feels so perfect. It wasn't until twenty years later that car guy Larry learned how perfect it was: Enzo Ferrari's first win as a driver came in the Parma-Poggio di Berceto hill climb.

With lease secured, design underway, and final name locked in, Larry selected the restaurant's opening chef-partner, Chris Fernandez, who had previously worked at Oliveto in Oakland, Cypress Club and Stars in San Francisco, and elsewhere. He and Larry worked together for more than a year before the restaurant opened. As part of his preparation Chris made several research trips to Italy, spending eight weeks working for Carlo Cioni at his famous Da Delfina restaurant in Florence.

Larry liked Chris and respected his ability in the kitchen. But there was one other factor that made him an appealing hire. Larry believed that the *San Francisco Chronicle's* influential restaurant critic, Michael Bauer, was a Fernandez fan.

In 1996 Bauer had introduced the *Chronicle's* Top 100 list, honoring restaurants he felt worthy of acclaim. Not a single Il Fornaio had ever made the list, possibly because of an understandable anti-chain bias.

If Bauer didn't want to consider some very fine restaurants because they were part of a larger family, that was his right. Fair enough. Still, it rankled competitive Larry. He thought several Il Fornaios were deserving. Other reviewers, including some of Bauer's own *Chronicle* colleagues, praised the restaurants enthusiastically.

Larry felt confident that his one-off, non-chain "dream restaurant" would be good enough to crack Bauer's Top 100 no matter who the chef, so long as they were up to Larry's standards. All else being equal, however, having Chris Fernandez on his team could only make it that much more likely.

Larry conceived and created Poggio while working out of his Il Fornaio office in Corte Madera, his experience this time almost the opposite of what he endured when restricted by the non-compete clause. Now it was more along the lines of, "You're going to start something of your own again? Great! How can we help? You need graphics? You know our graphics and design people, Hillary and Michael, from Il Fornaio's earliest days—why don't you use them?"

Mike Hislop set the tone and everyone else followed, a real tribute and act of generosity—though one that often paid dividends for Il Fornaio as well. Not every company had such an experienced and valuable resource just down the hall.

Poggio opened in November 2003. The room was beautiful, the food delicious, and for Larry "the drug had kicked in."

Overall, though, the first few months were, as Michael Mindel described in a 2023 twentieth-anniversary recap, "bumpy." Larry acted quickly and decisively, letting go Poggio's opening general manager mere weeks into her tenure, then enticing Spectrum and Il Fornaio stalwart Umberto Gibbin to save the day.

If the restaurant hadn't yet begun to operate with the smooth consistency it's known for today, early on there were encouraging signs, starting with Michael Bauer's February 15, 2004, *Chronicle* review, parts of which are worth quoting:

> At Poggio in Sausalito, you learn that Larry Mindel is a guy who gives more than is expected, a man who loves the finer things but who understands value. His new Italian restaurant reflects all this and more.
>
> Yet for all his many (Spectrum and Il Fornaio) successes, he always had that hankering to create a restaurant that broke out of the pack and reflected his refined sensibility…with Poggio…he's hit the mark.
>
> The interior, crafted by Arcanum Architects of San Francisco, is gorgeous, with terra-cotta paver tiles inset with marble, thick gold marble baseboards and gently curved arches lined with mahogany. The generously spaced tables and the luxurious finishes, which include mohair banquettes, reveal

quickly that Mindel is concerned about comfort.

When Bauer's Top 100 list came out that April, Poggio was on it—to stay. It's difficult to stop Larry once he sets his mind on something.

Bauer wasn't the only critic with good things to say. *Esquire* magazine's John Mariani named Poggio one of America's best new restaurants: "Sausalito has needed a good restaurant for a long time. It got a great one." Longtime food critic Patricia Unterman wrote in the *San Francisco Examiner*, "No Mindel restaurant has served better food," a big credit to Chef Chris.

Poggio stabilized under Umberto's steady hand in the two short but vital years he lent it his singular warmth and professionalism. In 2006 he departed to open his own restaurant, the very successful Perbacco, in San Francisco on California Street, next door to the Tadich Grill. As a mentor, friend, and investor, Larry has been delighted to see Umberto and his wife Leslie do so well with Perbacco.

Bartender Tony Di Iorio was another of "Larry's guys." Known to some as "Tony Negroni," after the famous Florentine gin-vermouth-Campari cocktail—he mixed hundreds of thousands in his long and illustrious career—Tony first started working with Larry at Prego in 1985.

Larry and longtime Prego and Poggio bartender Tony "Negroni" Di Iorio

Tony hadn't wanted to work in his family's restaurant, so at eighteen he left his home region of Cinque Terre on the Italian Riviera. He wandered for a bit—Beirut, Iran, Belgium, cruise ship work in the Bahamas, and even back to Italy for a spell—before landing at Prego, where he soon became an institution. He was even featured in a playful full-page, color print ad for the restaurant in *San Francisco Focus* magazine.

Tony continued to work at Prego long after Larry left. In 2003 his former boss, whom he referred to as "numero uno," called.

"I just signed the lease for a new restaurant, but I won't open it without you behind the bar," he said.

"When do you need me?"

"Tomorrow."

"I'll be there."

Tony quit Prego that night and reported to Poggio the next day.

In a favorable September 2004 review, Southwest Airline's in-flight magazine called the restaurant "a piece of Italy, from the terra cotta floor to the Carrera marble bar. But the most Italian thing about Poggio is Tony, the barkeep from the old country."

Scores of Poggio regulars "come for Tony." His following rivals that of his beloved Elvis Presley. When asked if he is Italian, Tony likes to answer with that trademark twinkle in his eye, "No, I'm Norwegian," before breaking into gibberish that he says is "Love Me Tender" in Norwegian.

Loving Tony as he does and clearly seeing Tony's significant contributions to both Prego and Poggio's success, Larry made him a partner in the Sausalito restaurant.

Larry couldn't distribute partner shares to all his employees. But he could take the time to learn their names and something about their lives, something done not as a Hug Your People technique from a leadership seminar, but as a natural expression of his extroversion and a genuine curiosity about and appreciation for people.

When Tom Hyde walks through the kitchen with Larry, he marvels at how many Poggio employees, from cooks to dishwashers, Larry truly knows. Tom also notices what he believes to be the real warmth that Poggio's employees feel for "Lorenzo"—not always the case in owner-worker dynamics.

In 2008 Larry hired Amy Svendberg as managing partner. She had worked in Paris and Chicago before coming to San Francisco's Grand Café. Amy and new chef Peter McNee worked well together. Even as the pair really began to hit their stride, however, forces outside the restaurant—national financial issues well beyond anyone in Sausalito's control—began to make their presence felt.

Olympus had sold the Casa Madrona to MHG Casa Madrona LLC in 2005, a joint venture between the Falor Companies and the Mitchell Companies. Guy Mitchell, listed as the owner of the Casa Madrona, eventually was sentenced to five years in prison for things he did in that capacity.

As United States Attorney Sally Quillan Yates explained, "Our nation's financial crisis was fueled in part by bank insiders and major borrowers whose greed led them to break the law. The conduct of these defendants (Mitchell was one) help pave a path to the shocking number of bank failures Georgia has experienced in the last ten years."

Mitchell, Integrity Bank of Georgia's largest borrower, bribed the bank's executive vice president, giving him more than $200,000 so he could draw more than $7 million from a loan that was supposed to be used for renovation and construction at the Casa Madrona. No work was ever done. Mitchell used the money "to buy an island in the Bahamas, travel by private jet, purchase Miami Heat basketball tickets, buy fancy jewelry and cars, and a mansion in Coconut Grove, Fla.," according to a November 6, 2013, press release sent out by the United States Attorney's Office Northern District of Georgia.

After Mitchell defaulted on his loan and Integrity failed, the Federal Deposit Insurance Corporation (FDIC) took over the Casa Madrona. They were Larry's landlord for a brief while, and a very good one.

The FDIC intended to put the hotel up for foreclosure auction—standard procedure, since loans usually require collateral, a hard asset the lender can sell if an owner defaults on the loan. But Mitchell fought hard to hold on.

People gathered on the San Rafael city hall steps for the scheduled auction in August 2009. It was canceled at the last moment when Mitchell filed for Chapter 11 bankruptcy. His filing postponed the auction until October.

None of this affected Poggio much—not yet. Amy and Peter still performed exceptionally, food and service were superb, and business was good. But Larry and Tom began to wonder: *What if we bought the hotel?* Intrigued, they ran some numbers and figured out their opening and final bids for the October auction.

The partners coolly held to their predetermined maximum and were easily outbid for the hotel. The new owner was MetWest Ventures of Los Angeles, headed by Richard Hollander, who began his career at Drexel Burnham Lambert. Hollander was no stranger to significant sums. In 2010 he sold his Malibu house—previously owned by entertainer Don Rickles, known for his insult comedy—for $30 million.

After the auction, good sports Larry and Tom invited winning-bidder Hollander and his lawyer to lunch at Poggio, breaking bread together to inaugurate the new landlord-tenant relationship. Minutes into what Larry and Tom thought would be a pleasant midday repast, Hollander's lawyer peremptorily announced that Poggio's lease was way under market value and would be revised to current market terms.

This didn't make sense to the Northern Californians. A lease was a lease, and Poggio had many years left on theirs. It wasn't Larry's fault that Olympus had agreed to the Nonno Deal. MetWest saw it differently. They felt that the original lease had been terminated when Mitchell filed for bankruptcy.

The conflict was put to the side briefly, while Larry and Debby went on a memorable adventure.

After the Il Fornaio sale to BRS, Larry commissioned shipbuilders Cheoy Lee Yachts to build his dream boat, an 80' cockpit motor yacht.

He took three separate in-and-out trips to the shipyard in Hong Kong while the boat was being built. He enjoyed making the boat really *his*, weighing in on the many finishing details: fabrics, art, fishing setups, electronics, *Piccolo Mindy* (the boat's tender, or dinghy). He was particularly excited about the *Mindy's* club-grade sound system, which would enable him to play "Jimmy Buffet all day, every day. Guests would get sick of it, but I never did."

Larry loved life aboard the boat, the crown jewel of a succession of several *Mindys*. By the time he sold it in 2020, he had put 9,000 hours on the engines. He joked that boats were similar to restaurants for him.

"They're another sickness. But when I step onto that boat, I become the happiest man alive. All my problems disappear. It's a safety valve, an escape."

Larry and Debby's 2010 cruise of a lifetime was a 7,000 nautical mile voyage: Sausalito to Mexico, Mexico to Costa Rica, Costa Rica through the Panama Canal, Belize, and on to the Bahamas for Melissa Siebel's wedding. Friends Bill and Holly Green and Tom and Judy Hyde joined them for different stretches. John and Glennis Jones were there for the passage through the canal. Susan Fletcher put together a beautiful picture book memorializing the unforgettable odyssey, which Debby shares with anyone wishing a look.

Larry had barely regained his land legs when he learned MetWest had filed a lawsuit to evict Poggio, based on the claim that the Mitchell bankruptcy had cancelled Poggio's lease.

Larry was steamed. Many of his friends suggested he suck it up and pay the new rent to avoid losing the restaurant. Something didn't feel right about that to Larry.

After a solo trip to Montana focused exclusively on figuring out what to do about the mess and helpful discussions with Tom Hyde and trusted confidant Dino Cortopassi (the "larger than life, force of nature" Central Valley farmer and food processing magnate whom Larry had met in YPO), Larry felt energized. After the discussions, he had "a fresh pair of balls" and decided to fight back.

As Gary Klein's October 2, 2010, article in the *Marin Independent Journal* explained:

> Poggio recently sued the Casa Madrona Hotel and Spa in Marin Superior Court on claims of wrongful eviction, breach of lease, breach of covenant of quiet enjoyment, trespass and interference with prospective economic advantage.
>
> Poggio's action came two months after Casa Madrona filed a lawsuit against the restaurant, claiming it has not been paying its rent.
>
> ...The dispute dates to February, when the 63-room hotel, at 777 Bridgeway, changed hands in a foreclosure auction. A private equity firm in Southern California bought the hotel from the Federal Insurance Corp. and hired Terra Resort Group to run it.
>
> Poggio, a venture led by the Sausalito-based restaurateur Larry Mindel, has been operating on the ground floor of the hotel since 2003. According to Poggio's lawsuit, Casa Madrona's new management launched an unsuccessful attempt to evict the restaurant.
>
> 'Poggio was not in any way in default under its lease,'

wrote Michael Baker, a San Francisco lawyer representing the restaurant. (The hotel's) transparent purpose was to wrest possession and control of a multi-million-dollar restaurant space for free.'

Having failed in its efforts to evict the restaurant, Poggio claims, the hotel 'embarked on a new strategy.' The lawsuit says Casa Madrona 'engaged in a series of escalating acts to harass Poggio into either giving up the premises or agreeing to substantially higher rent.'

Among other allegations, Poggio claims the hotel forced the restaurant to pay valet parking for hotel guests as well as restaurant guests; filled Poggio's banquet and meeting rooms with office equipment; denied Poggio access to valuable event space and revenues; refused to pay for repairs on the property; and denied Poggio employees use of the parking lot.

Poggio is seeking $200,000 in damages from Terra Resort Group, injunctive relief, a rent reduction to cover economic damages, unspecified punitive damages and legal fees.

It was a matter of principle for Larry. He was from the Heartland, where a handshake was a handshake and a lease was a lease. He believed that MetWest had behaved similarly in at least one other instance, trying to squeeze out a leaseholder after buying the building it occupied. More generally, he was fighting for "all the small businesses facing landlords with deep pockets." He wasn't shy publicly, on October 7, 2010, telling Paolo Lucchesi of the *Chronicle's* online outlet *SFGATE*, "Bullies really piss me off, so I thought we would stand our ground and file a lawsuit."

The next few months wore on Larry. He wanted to feed people, not sue them. He stuck to his guns and was vindicated in March 2011 when the judge ruled in Poggio's favor, prompting some fun press coverage.

The March 10, 2011, headline on Jay Barmann's online "Grub Street" site column read, "You Go to War with Restaurateur Larry Mindel, You Lose." Barmann concluded his post with, "Take note, all who'll listen: You do not mess with Larry Mindel."

That same day Lucchesi wrote on *SFGATE*, "Happy endings:

Score one for the little guys: Sausalito's Poggio has won the lawsuit against its landlord, the Casa Madrona Hotel group. The two parties have been entangled ever since the hotel served the restaurant with an eviction notice last year. Poggio proprietor Larry Mindel fought it in court, claiming the eviction notice was unlawful and wrongful. Turns out the judge agreed with him, and Poggio plans to enjoy the next 19 years of its lease."

All was not immediately sunshine and lollypops after the ruling, however. In what Larry and Tom felt was part of the hotel's overall strategy of harassment, the Casa Madrona began to interfere with Poggio's exclusive right to provide food and beverages to the hotel, as stipulated in the lease. After less adversarial efforts to resolve the conflict failed, Dino encouraged the partners to file another lawsuit. His 2022 obituary noted "Dino was feisty, a David more than willing to take on any Goliath. In 1969 he sued giant Libby, McNeil and Libby Fruit and Vegetable Cannery for breach of contract and won."

Larry and Tom took Dino's advice. They sued the Casa Madrona for interfering with Poggio's exclusive right to provide food and beverages to the hotel. Legal fees mounted quickly however, especially since the Casa Madrona had appealed the judge's ruling in Poggio's favor and was withholding payment of the $520,000 attorney fees and costs. Larry and Tom believed the appeal was meritless, just more harassment. They also believed in the righteousness of their argument. Their suit was about money; but it was also, for Larry in particular, about right and wrong.

Larry was so convinced Poggio would prevail that he made the rather unorthodox decision to invite any of his interested partners to join the fight. Larry could have funded the suit himself, but once he realized that the withheld $520,000 was accruing 10% interest, he elected to raise that exact amount from willing partners, in the form of a short-term loan at that same, very attractive rate of interest. The loans were to be repaid immediately upon conclusion of the legal proceedings.

The situation could not have turned out better for Larry and his partners, almost all of whom chose to participate in the undertaking. Things moved quickly. He announced the loan opportunity in December 2011. Within little more than a week it was fully subscribed.

By February 2012 a Marin County Superior Court judge had

ruled in Poggio's favor. The next step would have been a jury trial for damages, but both sides opted for a settlement conference instead. The judge acted as go-between, shuttling from one room to another—*That's your number, here's their number, how about this one in the middle*? Back and forth negotiations went, until a vindicated and relieved Larry said, "We'll take it."

Everyone affiliated with Poggio shared in the victory. Partners who lent money got their stake back with interest, and the damages awarded helped make that year's distribution unusually robust. Employees received bonuses.

A significant distraction had finally vanished. Every team member, from Larry on down, could get back to focusing on what they knew and did best, running an excellent restaurant. The relationship between the hotel and Poggio became cooperative rather than adversarial, helped along by MetWest owner Richard Hollander's order to his staff: "From now on, we're all going to get along. The Casa Madrona will get along with Larry, the Casa Madrona will get along with everyone associated with Poggio." Going to work was soon a lot more pleasant for all.

That might have been the end of the story, except for an amusing postscript.

Several years later, Larry's youngest son, Nick, became business school buddies with Adam Hollander, Richard's son. One barbecue at Adam's apartment, the boys decided to tease their fathers on FaceTime: "Hi, Dads, it's us, Adam and Nick, just hanging out, having a great time." The implication clearly being, *you older guys might have been litigious rivals, but—look at us—great friends!*

In early 2013 chef Peter McNee left Poggio to start his own restaurant in San Francisco. Youthful, high-energy Ben Balesteri, who grew up hunting and fishing the Central Coast, took over from Peter and remains at the helm today.

Thanks to Ben and Amy—and Michael Mindel, who left Il Fornaio in 2017 to join Larry in Sausalito—and all their capable, dedicated staffers, more than twenty years on, food and service at Poggio have never been better nor revenue higher. For original investors, Poggio has generated a return on investment of more than 200%, roughly 7.5% annually. That's better than Treasury bills, if slightly less than the stock market. Not bad for a fun, buyer-beware crapshoot.

In 2015 the restaurant received the prestigious Michelin Guide's Bib Gourmand, a commendation near and dear to Larry's "affordable luxury" heart and mission to provide the "best value for money" and the leave the "diner with a sense of satisfaction for having eaten so well at a reasonable price."

The Nonno Deal included Larry's somewhat unheard-of no-minimum-rent provision: he would only pay a percentage of sales to the landlord each month, rather than the standard baseline minimum plus a portion of sales. This became extremely significant during the early months of Covid.

Poggio was closed. It wasn't making money. However, unlike almost every other restaurant out there, Poggio didn't have to pay rent. Money from reserves that would have gone to keeping the lights on could go instead to idled employees.

Larry always strived to make his restaurants a family, believing that the biggest key to his success was workers who "consider the restaurant home."

Poggio Managing Partner Amy Svendberg, Larry, and Chef Partner Ben Balesteri

Copita

In 2010 Kurt Krechel, a Poggio regular, invited Larry to take a look at his shuttered restaurant a few doors down on Bridgeway. Kurt, a successful industrialist, had opened a small Italian restaurant, Piccolo Teatro. It never took off.

Krechel found out what so many rookie restaurateurs before him had found out: the restaurant business is like no other. Experience and success in other lines of work don't always transfer to hospitality. He hoped to salvage whatever might remain of his investment by selling the restaurant's assets.

The small space intrigued Larry. Its proximity to Poggio brought back memories of his very successful MacArthur Park and Ciao restaurants, just around the corner from each other. That setup worked so well. But he wasn't looking to open another restaurant. Poggio was his beautiful, wonderful, perfect swan song.

However, the space was basically ready to go. Weeks earlier it had been a restaurant. It had a kitchen, use permits, and a liquor license. With all that in place, and given the space's small size—just 1800 square feet—start-up costs and attendant risk were relatively low.

"If you get desperate," Larry told Kurt, "I'll take it off your hands."

Krechel declined with a smile.

When he didn't find another buyer, however, that changed. On July 31, 2010, he and Larry signed an agreement between Poggio and Piccolo Teatro that gave Poggio the exclusive right to engage in due diligence and negotiate the possible purchase of Piccolo Teatro's assets. The agreement didn't mean for certain that Larry would buy the restaurant, but it was a significant step in that direction.

As months passed, Larry and Tom Hyde's enthusiasm mounted as they researched the specifics that would come with a purchase. How long was the lease they would inherit? Who would be their landlord?

In what shape was the building, really? The answers were promising, giving rise to another question.

What to put in the space?

Larry's natural inclination had been to do something Italian, sort of a Poggio annex. Perhaps a pizzeria. Maybe a salumeria, an Italian deli, heavy on pork. Or a vinoteca, a wine shop.

When he mentioned these possibilities to Michael, who was still working for Il Fornaio, his son shook his head. He'd seen too many spin-offs and satellites fail. Larry agreed. Besides, the more he thought about it, the more he realized he actually wanted something that wasn't Italian. Then he recalled the MacArthur Park-Ciao synergy: two very different concepts had fed off each other, the whole considerably greater than the sum of its parts.

One day, on the short walk back up Bridgeway to Poggio, following yet another visit to the small but promising Piccolo Teatro location, Larry thought of his third-favorite country.

Maybe Mexican, he thought. *I don't know squat about Mexican though. Guaymus was so long ago. I'd need to find someone who knows Mexican.* He rifled through his mental address book. A name came to mind.

Larry and Joanne Weir had met at various food-industry functions. She was a former Chez Panisse chef who had written a James Beard Award-winning cookbook and hosted cooking shows nationally on PBS. Larry felt a connection. He had recently invited Joanne and her husband, Joe Ehrlich, to be his and Debby's guests on the *Mindy*.

Although versions of the story vary slightly, per the most reliable account, Joanne and Joe boarded the boat in Charleston, South Carolina, at the tail end of the big Panama cruise. After the Siebel wedding, Larry and Debby had headed north to Florida and made their way up the Intracoastal Waterway, eventually reaching South Carolina.

After their first day together, the couples freshened up and met for evening drinks on the *Mindy's* stern.

"How about a margarita? I make the best in the world," Larry proclaimed.

Joanne raised an eyebrow.

"Really? I make a pretty good margarita myself. I should warn you, though, I wrote *Tequila: A Guide To Types, Flights, Cocktails and*

Bites."

Larry thought for a moment.

"How about I make mine, you make yours, and we decide which is best?"

Joanne laughed and agreed.

Larry went first. His margarita, a "Lorenzo," was delicious—top-shelf tequila, shaken, served up—and packed a three-ounce wallop. Michael later deemed it a "tequila martini," one that would get a drinker wherever they wanted to be in a hurry.

Joanne raised her glass in approval, and set about mixing her version.

Lorenzo shaking it up: the contest that created Copita.

Larry took one sip and exclaimed, "Goddamn it, Joanne, how did you do that? That's the best margarita I've ever tasted!" He added, "We should do a restaurant together someday."

"Yes! Fantastic!" Joanne replied, "Of course we should!"

Months later, as Larry racked his brain—*who knows Mexican?*—Joanne was the first to come mind, based, more than anything else, on her one delicious margarita and the maritime fun the two couples had together.

Before her tequila book, Joanne had written *From Tapas to Meze: Small Plates from the Mediterranean*. But—as the title said—that was Mediterranean, not Mexican. As for restaurants, Joanne had never run one before.

"Hi, Joanne," Larry exclaimed, wasting no time giving her a call. "I found our spot!"

"Our spot? Our spot for what?"

"A Mexican restaurant. Remember the margarita contest on the boat? We said we'd do a restaurant together. I found the perfect place for it, on Bridgeway in Sausalito, a few doors down from Poggio."

Hardly sold on the idea, but curious, Joanne met Larry at the space. She, too, saw the possibilities: a small but warm and vibrant Mexican *tequilería* and restaurant. It could feature both partners' signature margaritas and a modern, fresh seasonal menu of her creation.

A concept and a powerhouse possible partner in hand, Larry moved ahead. By May 2011 he began to pencil out projections, huddling with Tom Hyde. They believed financing and execution would be relatively easy. The space was small. It came with an already-built kitchen that required minimal modification. They were confident they could create something along the lines of their Poggio limited partnership on a smaller scale, success once again breeding more success. Poggio's capable managing partner, Amy Svendberg, could expand her duties and handle the new enterprise's front of house.

On July 21, 2011, Larry signed an asset purchase agreement with Kurt Krechel. He, Joanne, Tom, and Amy got to work in earnest creating Copita Tequileria y Comida.

Taking full advantage of the existing long mahogany bar and fireplace, the team "transformed the space: terracotta beeswaxed walls, hand-painted Mexican tiles in twilight blue and white surrounding the fireplace, seafoam green translucent tiles lining the bar, dark wooden floors, a blue and white hand-embroidered Oaxacan tapestry above the banquette, and a commissioned painting of a *jimador*, the man who tends the agave fields (tequila is made from agave), by artist Jay Mercado centered on the wall."

Larry wanted a lighter, brighter atmosphere. He felt strongly that the restaurant's front wall had to go. He wanted to replace it with folding glass doors that opened onto a small sidewalk seating area. Doing so required a special permit.

In a heartening show of support, more than a dozen residents backed Larry and Copita at the permit hearing. Esta Swig, wife of Martin Swig, Larry's car buddy and California Mille founder, told the council, "Please let Larry blow out that wall and put a few tables out front. You'd be fools not to. He knows what he's doing. Look at Poggio! He is great for our town."

Similar to those Larry had taken to Italy for decades with chefs and managers, Joanne and Larry took "authenticity trips" to Mexico. They recruited talented Mexican chefs, with whom Joanne developed a fresh, regional menu: seasonal tacos and ceviches and tortillas made from scratch. An August 26, 2024, *SFGATE* article featured a more recent creation, a shrimp and flounder dish with "white peaches, red onions, cilantro and serrano peppers drizzled with mint tomatillo dressing and topped with plantain bacon."

Fittingly enough, Copita opened on May 5, 2012, Cinco de Mayo. Originally a day of remembrance in Mexico, the holiday marks its victory over the French in the 1862 Battle of Puebla. Over the past forty years, in the U.S. it's since become more of a generalized and bibulous celebration of Mexican culture, similar in its way to St. Patrick's Day.

Joanne got a rude if completely standard welcome to the restaurant business: a week before Copita opened, the chef quit—par for the course. Someone had to step up while the team found a new chef, so Joanne did. When she and Larry were brainstorming the restaurant, she certainly hadn't envisioned twelve-hour days running the kitchen. But when that's what was needed at the most critical moment in Copita's life, that's what she did.

The "small but mighty" spot continues to punch above its weight, consistently generating the highest volume of sales per square foot or per seat of any of Larry's restaurants—ever.

Convivo

Richard Gunner, Il Fornaio Carmel's landlord, approached Mike Hislop and Michael Mindel several different times in the mid-2000s, inviting them to open an Il Fornaio in his recently purchased Santa Barbara Inn. Gunner, pleased with the flourishing Il Fornaio-Pine Inn partnership in Carmel, hoped to replicate that same synergy a little farther south.

The men might have closed a deal were it not for the 2008 financial crisis. The hotelier made one final overture in 2013, ahead of the property's major overhaul. Michael and Hislop turned down the offer, with sincere regret. They valued the Carmel partnership just as much as Richard did, and they had grown to like and respect him over the years. But they felt Santa Barbara was a little too small and too far away for them to manage.

Richard called Larry. He was flattered but also passed.

"I'm sorry, Richard. You know how much I like you personally, and I really like doing business with you. But Santa Barbara is just too far. I'm not doing any new restaurants at this point in my life, and, if for some crazy reason I were to open one, it would have to be nearby. My new rule is all my restaurants must be within an easy drive. No more airplanes!"

As he often does for friends in the business he really likes, Larry added that he would be happy to consult on the project for free.

Somewhat unusually, Richard planned to build out the majority of the restaurant himself, rather than leave that expense and work to whomever eventually occupied the space. Larry gave Richard names.

"You've got to have Anthony Fish design it, and George Frederighi for kitchen, back of the house…"

Gunner reached a promising tentative agreement with successful Santa Barbara and Montecito restaurateur and Lucky Jeans entrepreneur Gene Montesano. It fell apart in 2015, halfway through construction.

Richard called Larry again, with more urgency this time, requesting that Larry at least come down to take a look.

"The hotel remodel's almost done," he pleaded. "We can't open without a restaurant!"

Because Richard was a true friend—the only non-family member to attend the 2009 Boys Town of Italy dinner at the Fairmont Hotel, honoring Larry as its Man of the Year—Larry agreed to travel south.

He and Michael got as far as the Centurion Club lounge at San Francisco International Airport (SFO) when they learned their flight had been canceled. Larry called Richard to apologize.

"As I said, no more airplanes. I guess it just wasn't meant to be. I'm so sorry, and good luck with your project."

"Please hold on," Richard answered, "Just give me thirty minutes—sit tight for thirty minutes. If I can't come up with something during that time, you can leave. But please give me a chance."

The slot was already blocked out on Larry's schedule. The delay meant more time with Michael, who was still working for Mike Hislop at Il Fornaio. Mike had let Larry "borrow" his son for the reconnaissance mission. The food and drinks at the Centurion were decent—and free—so why not? What was thirty minutes for a friend?

Richard quickly called back. He had chartered a plane. All Larry and Michael had to do was drive from SFO to the Oakland Airport, where plane and pilot awaited. Father and son looked at each other, shrugged, and laughed. The adventure was on.

Larry was impressed with the restaurant's design and location, just across from Santa Barbara's famed East Beach. Even as he stood in his fancy dress shoes on the bare dirt of what would soon be the hotel lobby, he could tell the place could be a winner.

"You like it, Larry?" said Richard. "Write your lease."

Returning home, Larry felt a familiar surge, one he had assumed he'd never feel again after Copita opened in 2012.

"When I walk in, and the restaurant is packed, there's an hour wait, my heart goes boom, boom, boom," he later explained, smiling. "There's nothing else like it. It's just a sickness."

He and Michael saw that, although distance would be an obstacle, the project was feasible. It even had some notable things going for it, not least of which was their comfort with Richard. Furthermore, experience told them that negotiating a lease—as with Poggio, Larry would insist on free parking for his guests—would be as straightforward as it could ever be. Initial investment cost and risk would be relatively low, thanks to the already-built kitchen and beautiful dining room. And, Richard assured them, if it didn't work out, they could walk away at any time.

In the days that followed, Larry gave more thought to the fact that two of his three later-years non-negotiables were already in place: a landlord he liked, and a place where he would want to spend time. The third was a partner or partners with whom he wanted to do business.

In what had become a fairly regular, if still bittersweet, occurrence over the course of his career, Larry had bid Poggio Executive Chef Peter McNee a warm, grateful, sad goodbye in early 2013. Peter was another of dozens of key employees or partners who, having learned and grown with Larry, got the "sickness" themselves and left to open their own places. Nick Nahigian, a Poggio manager and wine buyer, left along with Peter.

The two began to scout San Francisco locations. The process dragged out. They would find a possible location, but lease negotiations would hit a snag. Peter began to consult. He spent time in restaurant kitchens and offered professional advice, helping establishments improve their operations. He even picked up some shifts as a line cook at Rose Pistola. Meanwhile, Nick hooked on with Umberto at Perbacco. Peter and Nick did whatever it took to make ends meet as they worked to open their own restaurant.

When Larry heard it was taking Peter—who had done great things at Poggio—longer than anticipated to get started, he thought *that's my chef-partner for Santa Barbara.*

Peter and his wife Rachel were intrigued when Larry floated the idea. They were willing to take a look, though sensibly noncommittal at first. Peter had been completely focused on conceiving and running his own restaurant in San Francisco; a partnership in Santa Barbara would be a significant pivot. After a trip south to look at the restaurant coming together in the under-renovation Santa Barbara Inn, they realized that they and their newborn, Firth, might really benefit from the move. Peter and Rachel signed on.

Larry was delighted. He knew and trusted landlord Richard. The location was beautiful. And he felt great about the strong ownership team that was coming together: Larry; Peter; Amy Svendberg, who would now oversee not just Poggio and Copita but the Santa Barbara outpost as well; Tom Hyde; and, in a dream come true for Larry, son Michael.

Although Michael still worked for Il Fornaio, CEO Mike Hislop fully supported the new father-son endeavor. Hislop knew that Michael had long been and would continue to be a loyal and conscientious executive who always put his primary employer's interests first. What Michael did outside of that, on his own time and dime, was up to him.

Larry and Peter decided upon the name "Convivo," the Latin term for "feast." Peter described his style of food for the restaurant as "Nomad Italian…the foundation—our soul—is Italian, but our destination is Santa Barbara. The menu draws from different styles and traditions along the way."

Convivo opened in the summer of 2016. Business was choppy at first; the hotel wasn't finished yet. Things began to pick up, but 2017 and 2018 were years of natural disasters: horrendous fires—Michael remembers driving down Highway 101 as flames swirled on both sides of the freeway—followed by the Montecito mudslides that killed twenty-three people. The hotel filled with well-heeled evacuees, but closed roads made it difficult for kitchen and wait staff to get to work. Scheduling and shift coverage were nightmares.

The restaurant began to find its way in 2019, helped by a small but strong piece in the *New York Times,* only to get knocked back again in 2020 by Covid. Yet while Convivo regulars and workers were not spared on a personal level, in a strange and fortuitous twist, the restaurant itself benefitted from the pandemic.

Convivo's large patio allowed staffers to devise and implement a "safe seating" plan, which provided more than the legal amount of space between the outdoor tables. It also had the unintended consequence of acting as a very effective billboard. Motorists would pass by and see that the restaurant—unlike so many others—was not only open but also safely filled up. Word spread, business nearly doubled that year, and Convivo never looked back. It's still thriving today.

Part-owner Michael was extremely involved in Convivo, from conception to opening to early-days management. In the midst of that remarkably busy time, when he was giving his all to Il Fornaio while also still collaborating with Larry, Peter, and Amy down south, Michael somehow found time to contemplate his future.

Larry loving life: celebrating son Tony's 50th birthday at Convivo; Santa Barbara, CA, 2019.

He had been at Il Fornaio for more than twenty-five years, and he had loved almost every minute of it. All the same, sometimes he thought about the remaining ten or fifteen years of his career. Would he keep doing what he'd long done, as satisfying as it was? Or, should he "repot" himself, as Larry had done several times, and finish by doing something different?

Michael talked with an old friend who was a very successful food businessman. The two brainstormed what it might be like for Michael to join the friend's company.

Although Larry wants nothing but the best for his children and grandchildren, and would never stand in the way of any loved one's personal growth, nothing pleases him more than having everyone close. At one point all five of his children and their families lived within fifteen minutes of their beaming patriarch. So, when Larry heard about the possibility of Michael leaving Il Fornaio, he had mixed feelings. He understood well the draw of a stimulating new challenge—he himself had pursued many over the course of his career. At the same time, he did not like the idea of his son leaving the area, a possibility if Michael signed on with his pal.

Larry mentioned his dilemma to his trusted CPA and tax advisor, Kamran Ghiasi.

"Larry, you're eighty years old," Kamran began. "What if you gave your very well-qualified son the opportunity to succeed you in your business? Do you think that might keep him local?"

Larry wondered why he hadn't thought of that himself. It seemed so obvious. And perfect—to him at least.

When he mentioned the possibility to Michael, he thanked Larry, expressed interest, and admitted that the possibility had crossed his mind once or twice.

After taking some time to think it over, Michael accepted Larry's offer, provided he could do so in a way that worked for him. His plan was to leave Il Fornaio and open Restaunomics, "a restaurant management and consulting company created to help independent and multi-unit restaurants navigate the unprecedented challenges facing the hospitality industry, utilizing new ideas about customers, sales and marketing." Restaunomics' primary clients would be Poggio, Copita, and Convivo, but having his own shop would enable Michael to work with other entities as well.

Larry was delighted. Michael left Il Fornaio and opened Restaunomics on January 1, 2017. Father and son were already "back in business" with Convivo in 2016, but the new setup again saw them working side by side on a daily basis, as they had for so many years at Il Fornaio—a development they both loved.

Copita Willow Glen

Larry's last restaurant hurrah appears to be Copita Willow Glen in San Jose, which opened just before his eighty-sixth birthday in October of 2023.

In 2020 he and Joanne were approached by developer Michael Van Every, president of Republic Urban Properties. Van Every wanted to build his corporate headquarters next to the best Mexican restaurant he could imagine. He searched for it for quite some time before finding Copita in Sausalito, whereupon he knew *this is it, this is the restaurant we want.*

Van Every asked Larry and Joanne if they would open a Copita in the two-story building he planned to put up at the corner of Lincoln and Willow, once the site of a gas station. Inspired by the architecture of Mexico's colonial-era San Miguel de Allende, he wanted to build something special.

In an interview with *SFGATE*, Michael, speaking for Larry and Joanne, said that when Van Every made his inquiry, "We looked at him like he had two heads. Opening a new restaurant during Covid? No, thank you."

But when Joanne visited the neighborhood, she really liked it. What's more, the plans for the new building impressed her. They called for two stories, two kitchens, and two bars. She was amazed.

She, Larry, Michael, Amy, and Tom began to ponder. The original Copita in Sausalito benefitted from a low opening cost, thanks to the previous restaurant tenant's build-out. A small overall footprint had forced them to keep things simple—and profitable. *SFGATE* pointed out that Copita Sausalito "hummed along, thanks to a pristine waterside location, and an international clientele familiar with the kind of fresh, regional cuisine they were pushing out."

Willow Glen would be a very different situation. A brand-new building requiring full restaurant build-out. A space 6,000 square feet that, when complete, would be triple the size of its North Bay forerunner. Two stories, two kitchens, two bars, and a large private dining room. Great sunsets from the rooftop firepits, but no bay, no international tourists.

Could it work?

They decided to take the chance, Larry swayed in part by the opportunity for three generations of Mindels to work side by side: Larry, Michael, and Michael's son Dashiel, who would be the restaurant's marketing manager.

When pandemic-related permit and supply-chain delays tested the team's resolve, it truly seemed that they were relying on a "triumph of hope over experience." They knew better, after all. Trying to open a restaurant during Covid was ridiculous. There was a reason that they had initially looked at developer Van Every as though he had two heads. They nevertheless stayed the course and opened a stunning showplace.

As Republic's website described:

> Copita is a visual feast, from the colorful depiction of San Miguel de Allende in an outdoor mural to the tile pattern indoors that was inspired by a wall Weir spotted while exploring Oaxaca. Anthony Fish of Arcanum Architecture headed the design project and created the look that features a vibrant teal wall and tiles and copper-top bar downstairs. Upstairs there are whimsical tiles and a white oak bar. A large *trompo*—the vertical spit from which executive chef Azari Cuenca-Maitret, a culinary star from Mexico City, and his chefs carve roasted meats—enjoys a place of honor nearby…Diners should see some spectacular sunsets from the rooftop patio, which faces west. Below and to the south are the lights of busy Lincoln Avenue. A private dining room upstairs has views of the Santa Cruz Mountains.
>
> The food is modern Mexican: choice ingredients and California produce in regional Mexican recipes. All sauces are made in-house, from the moles to the salsas, as are the chips and tortillas. Seafood and meat share starring roles…Dessert

choices include Mexican doughnuts, buñuelos, filled with *cajeta*, dusted with sugar and fried with a Oaxacan chocolate sauce.

Copita backs up its 'tequileria' name with dozens of tequila and mezcal options and also boasts a full bar. Each of the signature cocktails comes with its own special flourish: The large square ice cube in the Copita Margarita, made with Herradura Silver, is etched with the restaurant's name. A mini loteria game card is attached to the rim of the Loteria, a refreshing concoction of Tanqueray Sevilla, lemon, orgeat and passion fruit. And the Mangonada cocktail, Smirnoff Spicy Tamarind with mango syrup and lime, is served in a piece of hand-painted Mexican pottery.

Before the Copita Willow Glen doors opened that first night, the full staff gathered around Larry. He gave his trademark opening charge, which included in part:

> There are really three parts to restaurant creation. The first part is having a dream of what the restaurant could be.
>
> The second step is signing the lease to actually go from dream to reality.
>
> Here's where you staffers come in. We are about to take the third and final step and that is, to open our doors, deliver fantastic food, and create an atmosphere of camaraderie and excitement. It's not easy to bear the responsibility of this third and final step. In effect, I am giving you the keys to the car and the hope that you will drive it carefully. You are the real and most critical connection between the restaurant and the guest. All of us at Copita have put our trust and dreams in you.
>
> This is a family business, and you are now part of OUR family. Thank you all!

If Larry's days on the court and field were behind him, at eighty-six years old, the life he had made for himself still included peak-adrenaline pregame moments. The words he spoke that afternoon were solid but unspectacular; most meaningful to those like Michael who had worked with Larry for so long. He had heard that same "keys to the car" metaphor at dozens of previous openings.

Larry's charismatic presence and delivery had more of an impact than the words he spoke. In some ways, boiled down to its simplest essence, a leader is just someone whom others will—or *want to*—follow. Leaders can have all the great, visionary ideas in the world, but if they don't reach people in a gut, visceral way they'll never really lead—at least not as effectively as Larry has for more than seventy years, going all the way back to his student government and athletics days at Ottawa Hills High School. He's got soul.

As does Mike Hislop, whom one restaurant industry insider described as "ruggedly authentic." Far from a sycophant, Hislop doesn't traffic in superlatives. But when he attended the Willow Glen opening with his wife Laura—they are part of the restaurant's limited partnership—he gave Larry a handwritten birthday card, part of which read:

> You are truly one of the most amazing and talented men I have ever met. I feel blessed to have worked with you and honored to be one of your friends. <u>sincerely appreciate</u> our relationship and your <u>mentorship</u>. I hope you have a fantastic birthday celebration with your family and friends…nice to have another restaurant opening on your birthday weekend. We've done this before. I'm sure Copita Willow Glen will be a huge success. Love you, Larry. Mike.

Finito

At eighty-seven, the little Jewish boy from Toledo marvels when he reflects back upon his remarkable life.

"Are you kidding me? The way it all turned out? I couldn't be more fortunate. That's why I don't want to die. It's not that I'm scared. I just love life too much."

Toby Keith's "Don't Let the Old Man In" is one of Larry's favorite songs. A golf course conversation with Clint Eastwood prompted Keith to write it. He asked the actor how he planned to celebrate his upcoming eighty-eighth birthday, to which Eastwood responded he was going to go shoot a movie. Keith, in his late fifties at the time, laughed and asked how a man almost ninety years old could remain as active and alive as Clint clearly was. Eastwood thought for a moment, then said, "I try to get up and be productive, and don't let the old man in."

Inspired, Keith began to write the song that night. He sent it to the actor, who ended up using the song in *The Mule*, the movie he was shooting.

Don't let the old man in
I wanna live me some more
Can't leave it up to him
He's knocking on my door
And I knew all of my life
That someday it would end
Get up and go outside
Don't let the old man in
Many moons I have lived
My body's weathered and worn
Ask yourself how old you would be

If you didn't know the day you were born
Try to love on your wife
And stay close to your friends
Toast each sundown with wine
Don't let the old man in

One light but perhaps still telling example of Lorenzo's unflagging *entusiasmo per la vita* happened late one afternoon well after the birthday celebration.

As he left for the day, Larry heard the buzz of happy conversation from an office a few doors down. He poked his head in. Several young professionals, drinks in hand, stopped their conversation and looked over at the nattily attired octogenarian, as if to ask, "Can we help you?"

"Hi! You look like you're having fun," Larry said. "Who are you? What do you do?"

They laughed and invited him in, explaining they were enjoying their renewable-energy-finance firm's holiday party.

"Well, I'm Larry, and I own Poggio."

"It was so sweet," one of the firm's associates recalled. "He acted like everyone knew and loved Poggio. Not all of our colleagues were familiar with it—one of our newer hires thought it was a software company—but he was clearly so proud of his creation. And honestly, our generation, not too many people want to crash a party, let alone know how to do it with style, as Larry did. He was great."

Larry has taken risks all his life. A photo of a boat at anchor, along with the John Shedd quotation, "A ship in harbor is safe, but that is not what ships are built for," hangs on Larry's office wall. Rarely does workplace art capture the executive psyche as perfectly as that print.

Today Larry is loaded with post-victory satisfaction, amazement, and gratitude. Benevolence and magnanimity, too. Bygones have definitely become bygones. Any in-game animosity he may have once felt toward rivals or employees who went elsewhere or opened their own places was always temporary, a competitor's intensity, evaporated years ago.

He has long seen restaurants as four-legged stools: food, service, environment, and value. If a restaurant is missing one of those four legs it will teeter; if it is missing two it will fall over.

Larry considers marriage, family, work, and community to be the very stout four legs upon which his life rests. He is extremely grateful for the solidity of that base.

Debby never gets enough credit, he says, not just for her belief in and love for him as a man—without which he is absolutely convinced he would flounder—but also for her role as the matriarch, or "glue," of the twenty-three-person family they jointly head and cherish.

Full circle, back to the Big Island, from Caswell to today:
Larry, Debby, and all their kids and grandchildren; the Mauna Kea Beach Hotel, 2024.

Work has been chronicled here already. Larry's accomplishments have been recognized in many wonderful ways. In addition to the Caterina de Medici Medal, Larry also won the American Institute of Wine and Food's Achievement Award in 1990 and the *Nation's Restaurant News* Golden Chain Award in 1994. He was inducted into the California Restaurant Hall of Fame in 1998, the same year he also won the International Foodservice Manufacturers Association Gold Plate Award, considered by many to be the industry's highest honor. He was *Food Arts Magazine*'s Silver Spoon Award recipient in 2000, and, in something of a bookend to the 1985 Caterina de Medici Medal, he won the Carol Field Award for Italian Culture and Cuisine in 2020.

Il Fornaio inaugurated a Founder's Award in 1995, given each year to a manager who exhibits an entrepreneurial spirit, taking risks to improve the performance of their restaurant. The recipient "needed to make decisions as though he were a founder, balancing sales and profits, while ensuring that the brand was executed at a high level similar to that the diner would receive in Italy." The recipient also needed to show "the passion that Larry had for Il Fornaio and everything Italian." It was an emotional moment for Larry when he got to present the Founder's Award to one of the company's brightest young stars, Matthew Galli. Matthew's father was Franco Galli, the legendary *maestro*—and his *co-piloto*.

Matthew is not the only standout second-generation branch on the towering Larry tree: Tim Stannard, son of Larry's longtime Spectrum assistant and later Il Fornaio human resources chief Valerie Stannard, heads Bacchus Management Group, owners of Spruce, Village Pub, and Pizza Antica, among several other restaurants.

One additional tile in the occupational mosaic that brings Larry great pleasure: four of his five children have worked for his companies, in roles large and small: Michael is running the show now; Tony bussed tables at Guaymus; Katherine hostessed at Il Fornaio; and Nick parked cars at Poggio and managed Copita. Older grandsons have signed on as well: Dashiel as a Poggio host and now marketing manager for Copita Willow Glen; Sam at Copita's 49er game pop-up at Levi's Stadium; Al also as a host at Poggio; and Henrik as bartender at Copita.

Larry's work has consistently fulfilled him. That pleasure and satisfaction he derives, along with an innate generosity and desire to belong and give—time, talent, and treasure—radiates out, benefitting many. As Winston Churchill said, "We make a living by what we get, but we make a life by what we give."

Larry has employed thousands, fed millions, and mentored many.

"If you have a good attitude, my job is to mold you into a better restaurateur, even if you leave to start your own restaurant. Just at Il Fornaio we spawned over thirty new restaurant companies from people who graduated and moved on. I am happy for them—they achieved their dream. You have to want others around to succeed, or you won't succeed yourself."

Some of his restaurants have matured into true community gathering places and nerve centers, Poggio being a superb example.

Larry has also thrown countless benefits. In the words of long-time librarian and dean Brenda Brown, "For me, Larry is a marvelous man—a wonderful board chair who raised (with Mimi and Debby) wonderful children and was generous with us Branson folks, introducing us to each new restaurant at a gratis, slow opening. Donal and I were always delighted and grateful."

The Anti-Defamation League presented Larry with its Distinguished Community Service Award in 1993. The Boys' Town of Italy, a charity helping war refugee, migrant, and at-risk youth living on the streets of Italy, honored him as its Man of The Year in 2009.

Larry's has been a life well lived, a life true to himself, one in pursuit of his passions and in service to the many whom he has mentored, lifted up, and inspired to live their own best lives.

Grazie

This project began as an attempt to establish a simple timeline. Thank you, Larry, for "being open" to more once we started to talk in earnest. Although your grandchildren were always the intended recipients of this gift you're presenting—information, perspective, and revelation—as your son-in-law, I, too, have benefitted greatly from your offering.

I am hardly an authority on Larry Mindel, and I have no wish to horn in on your own sons' primacy, but thank you for the length and depth of our exchanges. Lines from another of your favorites, Jimmy Buffet's "The Captain and the Kid," come to mind:

> *I never used to miss the chance*
> *To climb up on his knee*
> *Listen to his many tales*
> *Of life upon the sea*
> *We'd go sailin' back on barkentines*
> *Talk of things he did*
> *The world was just a day away*
> *For the captain and the kid*

Socrates said that the unexamined life is not worth living; others have argued that the unlived life is not worth examining. What a span yours has been. Your colorful anecdotes have been gold to a kid raised on Caen and Conrad (Barnaby). Thank you.

I loved my own father and appreciated the conversations we had over the years. But even now, more than a decade after he died, I still yearn to know more about him. Being able to interview twenty of his family, friends, and associates would have been extremely interesting and satisfying. I now know that from firsthand experience, having had the tremendous privilege of doing so for you.

Gigantic thanks to all who gave so generously of their time and recall: Chuck Frank, Valerie Stannard, Gayle Blum, Gary Goddard, Steve Goddard, Mike Cinelli, Bill Higgins, Cindy Pawlcyn, Bill Upson, Doug Biederbeck, Stanley Morris, Marsha Guerrero, Umberto Gibin, Romano Chietti, Michael Dellar, Corinne Hedrick, Michael Mindel, Debby Mindel, Jonathan Sigal, Tony Di Iorio, Mike Hislop, George Frederighi, Tim Stannard, Matthew Galli, and Tom Hyde.

Special thanks as well to Larry's current assistant, Allyson Josephs, for her invaluable help. Not only did you folks take the time to talk, but, in many cases, you read over and made more accurate or just plain better my initial stab at your stories. I was aware of, or knew about, many of you growing up. Still, talking as we did over the course of this project, one ostensibly mature adult to another, has been an unexpected and delightful opportunity for me to finally sit at the grown-ups' table. Such a rush.

Larry wanted Cheryl Popp, owner of Sausalito Books by the Bay, onboard from the start. Now I know why. Thank you, Cheryl, for your insight, enthusiasm and tact. You improved the book greatly.

Cheryl also introduced us to Larry's fellow Ohio native, Matthew Félix, without whom *Lorenzo!* would be just a bunch of stapled-together pages from Kinko's. Thank you, Matthew, for taking this project from the abstract to the concrete and for doing so with style, professionalism, and wit.

And finally: thank you Laura, for always encouraging me to write and generously supporting my efforts to do so. *Grazie* as well for inviting me to join the circus, bringing me into the fun and loving embrace of your incredible family. What an adventure it's been…*amore e linguine per sempre, bella!*"

www.ingramcontent.com/pod-product-compliance
Lightning Source LLC
Chambersburg PA
CBRC091135130526
44582CB00033B/170